PLANT
ED
BABY

CW01661318

Welcome!

As vegetarianism and veganism become more popular, you may have adjusted your diet to include less meat and dairy products. Now you're a parent, you may wonder if it's possible to raise a happy, healthy baby on a plant-based diet.

This book gives you all the facts and skills you need to make sure your baby is weaned on a nutritious vegan or vegetarian diet and grows up to be a strong and healthy adult.

Follow @PlantBasedBaby_uk on Instagram for more ideas, advice and tips on a plant based baby diet.

About the author

Sally J Hall is Editor of a popular nationwide parenting magazine and a journalist who has, over her career, written for almost all the magazines and websites for pregnant women and new parents in the UK. She has a keen interest in helping new parents make sensible and ethical choices that are right for their families. She was a vegetarian for many years and decided to choose a plant-based diet eight years ago.

Sally is author of Eco Baby, A Guide To Green Parenting, published by Green Books and a contributing editor to Watch My Baby Grow, published by Dorling Kindersley.

Please be aware that the information contained in this book is designed to be helpful in your journey towards a vegan lifestyle with your family. It is not to take the place of medical or healthcare advice and if you intend to pursue a vegetarian or vegan diet for your baby, you should discuss this with your doctor or health visitor and consider seeking the advice of an infant nutrition expert. The information contained in this book is correct to the best of our knowledge at the time of publication. Please seek up to date medical advice and recommendations, as advice may change. Similarly, if you believe that your baby has a reaction to specific foods or if there is a family history of allergies, you should seek medical advice.

The author and publishers disclaim, as far as the law allows, any liability arising directly or indirectly from the use, or misuse of the information contained in the book.

With thanks to Paul

Plant Based Baby is published by Aveta Publishing Ltd 2020.

Text copyright © Sally J Hall
Photography copyright © Paul Alcantara

ISBN 978-1-5272-6268-3

Sally J Hall has asserted her right to be identified as the author of this Work in accordance with the Copyright, Designs and Patents Act 1988.

Contents

The recipes

Photography by Paul Alcantara

Chapter One

Weaning

What is weaning?

In the UK we use terms such as "weaning" and "starting solids" when neither of these truly reflects the swap from a baby changing from a milk-only diet to eating a wide range of foods. What you are actually going to be doing is gradually
introducing first foods to your baby, usually as a purée or as small, soft pieces of food, while still continuing to breastfeed (or if you have been unable, or have chosen not to breastfeed, continue to offer your baby's usual milk).

The World Health Organization recommends that you start weaning once your baby has reached six months. The intention is not just to help your child make the change from your milk alone to eating a normal, adult diet but also to start to
introduce a wider range of nutrients that your child needs for healthy growth. The NHS also states: "Introducing your baby to solid foods – sometimes called weaning or complementary feeding – should start when your baby is around 6 months old."

Why shouldn't I wean my baby earlier?

Many people will tell you that their baby was 'ready' for weaning as early as four months; some will tell you that your baby will sleep through the night if you start to offer baby rice or similar. To add to the confusion, some pre-pre-pared baby food available in the shops says it is suitable from four months. So why does the NHS and the World Health Orgnisation say that six months is the right time to start?

- This protects baby's health by ensuring he is getting all the nutrients he needs from your breastmilk up to six months
- Weaning before six months can increase your child's likelihood of becoming obese in later life
- Your little one will be less at risk of stomach upsets if you wait to six months
- He is less at risk of aspirating food (inhaling pieces of food into the airways)
- His mouth and lips are well enough developed to be able to take food into the mouth, rather than pushing the tongue forwards, which a breastfed baby below this age will do

Weaning is a lovely process and can be great fun – but it can be quite challenging too, as your baby is, so far, unused to any tastes or textures beyond milk. The first time you give your baby a feed, you may find that most of it ends up on their face, in their hair and on their clothes – but don't worry, you'll both soon get the hang of it. Some babies take to it straight away, others take more time and each baby is different. Be guided by your little one and above all, keep calm.

Milk

Firstly, don't stop offering your baby their normal milk. You should start introducing food when your baby is awake and alert, when you are not in a hurry and when you have plenty of time. A teaspoon or two once a day may be enough at first; gradually you can begin to increase the amounts and the frequency with which you offer food. You may choose to start with baby rice or oats, or go for a single fruit or vegetable flavour. You could try offering the food halfway through a breast feed, so that your baby is not so hungry that they are fussy, but not too full to want to try it. Alternatively, try food a while after milk and before your baby is hungry enough for the next feed.

Turn to Chapter 7 for some ideas for the very first vegan and vegetarian weaning foods to try with your baby

How often can I introduce new flavours?

Try the first flavour for a few days in a row. When your baby is used to it and enjoying it, you can introduce another flavour at a different time of day or after the first flavour. Allow a few days for that one, then use this pattern from there. Babies tend to take a few tries to get used to flavours and textures, so don't assume your child just doesn't like a new taste. If she really seems to dislike it, you can stop that flavour and re-introduce it later on. Most parents seem to offer fairly bland tastes at first but don't assume your little one won't be interested in stronger tastes!

The next step

Now you can start to mix two flavours together. Once your baby has got used to this variety of tastes, you can then experiment further with more and more flavours. Try to choose ripe fruit and vegetables that are currently in season, as they will be at their most tasty and nutritious. They will also be more inexpensive! Locally grown produce is fresher and also results in fewer air miles, so makes a good ethical choice for you and your baby.

Some good first tastes are

Rice	Spinach
Oats	Quinoa
Potato	Polenta
Carrot	Sweetcorn
Apple	Broccoli
Pear	Parsnip
Peach	Courgette
Banana	Lentils
Avocado	Butter beans
Peas	Beetroot

These are all fairly bland and uncontentious flavours but perhaps your baby will enjoy more mature tastes. You can also start to introduce herbs and spices from quite a young age. The key is to experiment and to keep it interesting.

What should be in my baby's balanced diet?

You should aim to include these food groups once weaning is well established:

- Carbohydrates such as rice, grains, potato, cereals and bread
- Protein in the form of nuts, grains, beans and lentils
- Fruit of all kinds
- Vegetables of all kinds
- Plant-based milks with added calcium (not as an alternative to breastmilk but to mix with foods)
- If you are offering a vegetarian diet, include whole-milk cheese, yoghurt and other dairy products for their protein and calcium content.

You should also try to include as many colours of fruit and vegetable as possible, as these relate to the nutrients that are in fruit and vegetables; having a 'rainbow' of foods will ensure that a good range of vitamins and minerals are included.

If you have chosen a vegetarian diet, do not offer cow's milk as a drink until after one year of age.

What should I approach with caution?

Some foods can cause sensitivities and some can cause or exacerbate things like nappy rash. Strawberries and citrus fruits are good examples, so introduce them a little at a time; pause if they cause a reaction.

What should I avoid giving my baby?

- **Salt:** babies do not need extra salt and it can damage their kidneys if they have too much, so don't use any at all when cooking; check for salt content on any ready-made foods you offer.
- **Sugar:** similarly, do not add sugar as this can cause tooth decay; try not to offer foods that are high in sugar. Fruit juice should be diluted with water and only offered at mealtimes – not between meals. Natural fruit is a good addition to cereals if you want to sweeten it.
- **Honey:** This contains botulism organisms so shouldn't be given to babies. It's also a substance that many vegans avoid.
- **Tea and coffee:** your baby should not be given any drinks containing caffeine.
- **Fizzy drinks:** these should also be avoided as they contain high levels of sugar and acid and may also contain caffeine.
- **Nuts:** If you or your family have nut allergies, this is one food you'll want to approach with caution. You can offer nuts from six months but do so when you are going to be able to watch your baby's reaction afterwards. Interestingly, countries where babies are frequently given snacks containing peanuts from an early age seem to have fewer incidents of nut allergies. Watch your baby carefully when offering nuts, as they can be a choking hazard; cut up larger nuts.
- **'Diet" foods:** babies need whole fat milk, cheese and yoghurt, if you are including it in their diet. Don't offer low-fat versions.
- **Foods high in saturated fat:** avoid things like cakes, biscuits and crisps that have high levels of saturated fat, including some ready meals.

Other products that frequently cause allergies are milk and dairy products and eggs, so if you are weaning your child on a vegetarian, rather than vegan diet, ask your health visitor or a dietician for advice. Eggs can now be safely eaten lightly cooked if they have the British Lion mark. Those without the Lion Mark should be cooked until both the white and yolk are solid.

Eating as a family

Once your baby is enjoying a good range of foods and is eating reasonable amounts, it makes sense to offer food at the same time that everyone else is eating. This makes mealtimes with the whole family a normal thing to do and the example of seeing others eating will encourage your baby to eat too – they are extremely imitative!

Once you have a few healthy baby meals in your repertoire, you can start to make a meal for the whole family, of which a small portion can be set aside and puréed for your baby or chopped into small pieces if you are following the baby-led approach. Don't forget to take the baby's portion out before adding any strong flavours like chilli - but babies are surprisingly receptive to herbs and some milder spices!

How do you know if your baby is ready for weaning?

Your baby's immune and digestive system are ideally designed to get the most from breast milk alone for the first six months of life; it provides all the nutrients and fluids they need.

Then, as the muscles of the mouth and stomach improve, and they are able to sit up, they will start to be ready to accept food.

How can you be sure that your baby is ready for weaning? Here are some tips:

- Your baby should be able to sit up well in a highchair .
- They should be able to hold their head up steadily, so as to be able to pay attention to the food they are offered.
- They should have fairly good coordination by now and be able to pick up objects and take them to and from their mouth.
- They should be able to use fine motor skills – this means using their pincer grip to be able to hold small items. This is especially helpful with baby-led weaning.
- They should by this age have developed the ability to take food in the mouth and swallow it. Before this, babies have what is called the tongue-thrust reflex, where they push things out of the mouth.
- Your baby may now start to take an interest in what you're eating, grab your spoon and reach for your food.
- They may be chewing their hands and waking more frequently in the night and taking more milk.

Continuing along the weaning journey

Once you have established weaning and your baby is enjoying a few feeds a day, at meal times or in between as it suits you, you can begin to branch out a bit. If you started off with purées, you can introduce finger-foods and snacks in what is known as baby-led weaning, where your baby feeds himself from foods that you offer (see the recipe pages for tips on baby-led foods). Alternatively, you may have started off with baby-led foods.

There's no right or wrong way to wean, so do what suits you best and try both approaches, to see what your baby prefers. The smooth and soft foods you start off with can gradually have small lumps left in them and you can progress to foods that look far more like what adults would eat – and eventually, to offering your child the same foods all of you are enjoying.

Food safety and basic hygiene tips

1. It's important that you follow good food hygiene practices when feeding your baby, as a stomach infection, salmonella or other form of food poisoning can be very serious in a baby, who can become very ill very quickly.

2. Make sure you always wash your hands thoroughly before cooking and wash all fruit and vegetables before using.

3. Wash your child's hands before a meal – it will be a good lesson for life. They should also wash their hands after using the toilet and after touching pets or playing outside.

4. Don't use any out-of-date ingredients and discard any that look or smell as if they are past their best.

5. Keep your kitchen work surfaces and all areas where food is stored clean and keep pets away from food preparation areas.

6. Make sure you thoroughly wash all food preparation utensils and pots, as well as chopping boards.

7. Don't re-use food your baby has rejected and when you're cooking for your baby, make sure all food is well cooked, then cool it before offering it to your baby.

Chapter Two

A beginners' guide to feeding your baby on a plant-based diet

Whether you have always been vegan or vegetarian, are trying to cut down on meat, fish and dairy or are starting your food adventure now you're a parent, there's no doubt that it can be a little daunting to try to bring your child up on a completely plant-based diet.

You're not alone! There are thought to now be around 3.5 million vegans in the UK according to a survey by Comparethemarket.com – this is a massive spike since the Vegan Society reckoned there to be around 540,000 vegans in 2016.

Membership of the Vegan Society has seen a 24% increase from 2017 to 2018. Campaigns such as Veganuary have introduced the concept to many people and vegan food is more widely available around the country.

Is it difficult to wean your baby on a plant-based diet?

Commercial baby food is freely available in shops and supermarkets and there are more and more 'ready meals' for babies springing onto the shelves. However, very few of these, with the exception of first fruit and vegetable purées, are vegan or vegetarian. So, it might seem to be more difficult to wean a baby on a plant-based diet as you don't have the luxury of buying all your baby's weaning foods.

What you do have, however, is more control about what you put into your baby's brand new body. In days when we are facing one of the worst obesity epidemics ever, when some children are having as much sugar by their 10th birthday as they should have in 18 years, you are right to be concerned about what goes into your baby's weaning food. Making your own food for your baby, at home, ensures you have complete control over the ingredients and their quality and it also makes sure you're not inadvertently offering any food that's higher in salt and sugar than is preferable for your little one's health.

What doctors and dieticians say

The health professionals you'll be likely to come into contact with may give you cautious advice on raising a child as a vegan or vegetarian. That's great, as it is important to take good advice and to make sure your child has all the nutrients they need.

They will tell you that deficiencies can be a problem for some vegans and vegetarians, especially in iron, Vitamin B12 and iodine. However, with some careful planning and choices, it is possible to offer food higher in these nutrients, or to offer supplements to your little one to make up for areas that a plant-based diet may be lacking in. Be sure to take your health professional's advice and get your child weighed regularly to ensure they are growing well.

How can I convince my friends and relations that I am doing the right thing?

One of the hardest things new parents face is criticism – implied or explicit – from others. You only have to venture out with a baby who has pulled his socks off to find that people will tut and tell you "that baby will be cold." Most of us fume
inwardly rather than say: "Well I know that, but he has pulled his socks off 15 times and now we've lost them."

Choice of diet is another area where others around you feel the need to offer their own opinions on your choices, whether you have asked for them or not. Say that you are vegetarian or vegan and you'll often find friends and relations saying things like: "Well, you're not going to bring your child up like that, are you?" Or: "Aren't you going to let them make their own choice?" Even: "Isn't it cruel not to give your child meat?" and one of the best ones: "What if they want to go to McDonald's with their friends?"

It's great to have a few simple and quick explanations to hand when you meet these criticisms and to have thought them out beforehand. Take a look at chapter five to read more.

Do your reading

It is helpful to find a couple of well-established websites, articles and books to help you understand the various roles that vitamins, minerals, fibre, protein and more food elements play in your diet. We would suggest you take a look at the following:

- The Vegan Society (vegansociety.com)
- NHS (nhs.uk/live-well/eat-well/the-vegan-diet/
- NHS on vegan and vegetarian babies (nhs.uk/conditions/pregnancy-and-baby/vegetarian-vegan-children/)

Check the labels

Make sure you read the labels on everything you buy. Some products may have fish or small amounts of meat or dairy in them, or eggs. We have found surprising things like a syrup sponge pudding made from fish margarine, crisps with milk in them and sauces that contain fish sauce or shrimp paste.

Look out for ingredients derived from milk such as

- Casein
- Whey
- Lactose

Wine and beer is often filtered through a substance called isinglass, which is the dried swim bladder of a fish, especially cod. Look for wines labelled vegan – as a tip, biodynamic or organic wines tend not to be filtered through isinglass and can usually be considered vegan. Many breads and pastries contain milk and butter.

Look out for gelatine in foods – this is derived from the hoofs of animals and is used to literally gel together things likes mousse and puddings. Jelly is an obvious place this can be found. There are vegan substitutes you can look out for, such as agar agar and vegan jelly made from seaweed.

Things to know and trust

A vegan diet can be a whole and complete diet in itself. You do not need meat, fish or dairy for a balanced diet and it is possible, with some care, to get all the vitamins and nutrients you need from a plant-based diet

Being vegan can help you balance blood sugar more effectively – as long as you don't load up with sweet treats! Research also suggests it can help control blood pressure, reduce cholesterol and help lower rates of heart disease.

It can help control type 2 diabetes and some claim it helps prevent certain types of cancer – especially cancers such as those in the bowel which are now largely thought to be due to consumption of meats, especially processed meats.

Being vegan lowers your carbon footprint and is one of the most important things you can do to help the planet.

Feeding and raising animals requires huge resources. Vast fields of crops, using valuable land and water are needed to feed each animal when those fields could be used to grow food for humans instead.

The fields of crops needed to feed UK cattle is estimated to be about the size of Yorkshire. Animal farming also creates greenhouse gases.

Of course, for many, the primary motivation for going vegan is to avoid being complicit in the exploitation of, and cruelty to, animals. Most believe that sentient creatures have a right to life and that mankind should not be using animals for their own exploitation – especially when those animals are factory or battery farmed and treated badly.

Many will know of the cruelty that is daily practice in the meat industry – from putting pigs who have just given birth into cages where they can't move or turn, burning off chicks' beaks, castrating baby animals with no anaesthetic, the list of appalling practices is well known and you can research more if you like.

Even meat labelled as free range is not cruelty free and these animals are killed at the same slaughter houses as battery animals.

Increasingly, people are understanding the benefits for their health of going vegan; the British Dietetic Association recognises that veganism is suitable for all people of all ages.

Being vegan is a far more sustainable diet. This way of eating takes a third of the land used for the meat and dairy industry.

I have made the choice; what do I do now?

Firstly, take things slowly. The biggest mistake some people make is to cut out a food without working out what they can replace it with. Start to do your research before you make the shift, or do it slowly and surely. That way, you'll find some amazing recipes ad feel full and satisfied with your new food routine. If you are used to a typically British 'meat and two veg' sort of meal, it's not going to be very satisfying to take away the meat! Think about having meat-free days and gradually increase them. Eat at vegan restaurants and try to re-create the meal at home. Follow a few vegan food bloggers on social media or but a couple of recipe books. Be inspired and get help and advice from other. One great resource is to look up 'Veganuary' online, where you'll find lots of tips, advice and recipes for people making the change.

Swap it up

Make some swaps in your diet to gradually increase your commitment to a vegan lifestyle Choose oat, soya or other plant-based milk for your hot drinks and cereals. Have a vegan lunch from a sandwich bar when you're at work.

Will it affect how I feel?

Some people report odd reactions in the first couple of weeks of going vegan. Some will feel a bit tired, some low on blood sugar and shaky, some hungry all the time. Try to work out what's missing from your new diet that might make you feel that way but above all, relax and realise that any change to your body will have an effect and will settle down with time.

Isn't it very expensive?

Some will tell you that being vegan or vegetarian is more expensive than eating meat, poultry, dairy and fish. While it's undoubtedly true that factory-produced meat and chicken is incredibly cheap nowadays, you have to ask yourself how a farmer can manage to produce a creature such as a chicken, rear it, feed it and sell it to a supermarket or shops who can then sell it to you for £3. Shopping for organic fruit and vegetables may be more expensive but when you consider what you are putting into your body - and your baby's – you may well decide it's worth it. However, you can visit a local greengrocer and bring home food to feed the family for the day incredibly cheaply and can make it even cheaper if you, for example, use bulk bags of dried beans and lentils instead of tinned and if you shop cleverly.

Can I get some help?

The vegan community is very supportive. If you join a couple of groups such as the Vegan Society or social media groups, you'll always be able to find someone to tell you where you can find vegan chocolate, cakes, pies and sauces at a moment's notice! Take a look at our Instagram account to find ideas for recipes, too.

Chapter Three

What about the protein?

One of the most frequently discussed food topics you'll hear people asking vegans, and to some extent vegetarians, is: "but how do you get enough protein?"

The NHS says that: "your child needs one or two portions of protein-rich food every day to make sure they get enough. Good sources of protein for children who eat some animal foods are dairy, eggs and fish." It then goes on to discuss options for those who don't eat some animal products and tell us:

Plant foods that contain protein include:

- Beans and lentils, and food made from them, such as tofu, hummus and soya mince
- Seeds such as sunflower and linseed
- Finely ground nuts or smooth nut butters such as cashew and peanut

Luckily, there are plenty of delicious vegan foods that contain protein and so with a good mix of different foods and by keeping an eye on what your baby eats, you can easily get enough protein for their everyday diet.

Why does my baby need protein?

Protein is one of the essentials your baby needs to grow, as it is composed of amino acid-building blocks. Our bodies can't make essential amino acids, so we have to eat them. Protein is used to form muscles and bones, make hormones, fight illnesses and take oxygen around the body. It is also useful for growing and repairing the body. With this information, it's easy to see why your growing and developing baby needs protein and also why people get so concerned that they are getting enough.

How much do they need?

Reassuringly, a child only needs between 10 and 20 per cent of their daily calories to come from protein. Some experts say 15 per cent as an average is about right.

Here's a guide to the protein children need each day at different ages:

Seven to 12 months:	11 grams
One to three years:	13 grams
Four to eight years:	19 grams

How do I ensure my baby's meals have enough protein in them?

Your meals and those of your baby should contain a good mix of nutrients, including a source of protein. Think of the proportions like a plate divided into sections, where there a quarter is a protein and 'good fats' source, a quarter is carbohydrates consisting of good whole grains, then the remainder is fruit and vegetables. Vegan parents need to replace the meat, fish or dairy often shown on such illustrations (take a look online for 'my healthy plate') with a plant-based protein, vegetarians with this and / or a dairy alternative.

Hint: once you are offering your baby meals with different elements to them (as opposed to single fruit or veg purées), try to offer the protein-rich foods first. So, for example, if you have a lentil-based stew or burger, try to feed your baby with that first so that they are getting enough protein and they are not filling up on the carbs first. Try, though, to ensure they get a good mix of all the food on offer.

How much protein is in foods?

This shows you roughly how much protein is contained in some key foods that are easy to find, allowing you to make the decisions on what to include in each dish.

- 100g of tofu contains 8g of protein
- 80g of cooked red lentils has 7g
- 25g peanut butter has 6g
- 80g kidney beans or chickpeas has 6g

Did you know that protein can also be found in all of these foods?

Lima beans	Lentils	Kidney beans
Black beans	Soya beans	Soya yoghurt
Seitan	Peas	Sweet potato
Veggie burgers	Quinoa	Amaranth
Broccoli & Spinach	Chickpeas	Chia seeds
Almond butter	Artichokes	Potatoes
Black eyed beans	Oat milk	Wholewheat bread
Pinto beans	Almonds	Canellini beans
Vegan sausages	Tofu	Spirulina
Asparagus	Spaghetti	Jerusalem artichokes
Kale	Buckwheat	Pinto beans
Wild & brown rice	Bagels	Peanut butter
Tempeh	Oats	Brussles sprouts
Soya milk	Pistachios	Sunflower seeds
Cashew & Brazil nuts	Spelt	Nutritional yeast
Sweetcorn	Sorghum & Teff	Hemp & Linseeds

Chapter Four

Vitamin check and getting enough iron

When you are thinking about food for your vegan or vegetarian family, you'll already be aware that you and your little one need a certain amount of vitamins and minerals and you may also know that some work best in conjunction with each other; for example, iron is better absorbed when you have it with vitamin C, so you might want to have a glass of orange juice or a red pepper with your spinach.

It also helps to know which vitamins come from which fruit, vegetables, nuts, seeds and legumes, so there's a list later on. As a vegan, there are some vitamins and minerals that can be more difficult to obtain from your diet, so you may want to pay special attention to those or consider a child-friendly, good quality supplement.

Essential ingredients in your baby's diet

You don't need to add all of these elements at each and every meal but over the course of a few days, you should ensure that these ingredients are included in your baby's food.

Staring with the most important ones:

Iron

What it's for: this element helps our bodies made red blood cells, which are very important, as their main job is to carry oxygen around the blood stream to every part of the body. If we don't get enough iron, we can get a condition called iron deficiency anaemia, also known as just anaemia, which can lead to tiredness and shortness of breath, also palpitations; you may have pale skin, which you can see if you pull the lower eyelid forward – the inside of the lid should be red.

Where to find it: Iron can be found in a vegan diet in beans and nuts, apricots and other dried fruit, brown rice and wheat and other whole grains, soy bean flour and leafy green vegetables. It is also added to some breakfast cereals.

Other sources:

- fortified bread and cereals
- dark-green leafy vegetables like kale and spinach
- wholegrains; like wholemeal bread, brown rice, oatmeal
- lentils and beans, chickpeas
- tofu and quinoa
- dried fruit, such as apricots, figs, raisins and prunes
- Brewer's yeast and blackstrap molasses

B Vitamins

What they are for: This is actually a group of vitamins, including thiamine (B1), riboflavin (B2), niacin (B3), B6, biotin (B7), B12, folate and folic acid and pantothenic acid.

These have several beneficial effects on our bodies but broadly speaking, they help us break down food and release its energy, keep our skin, eyes and nerves healthy, help us store energy from protein, form haemoglobin and also formhealthy red blood cells.

Most importantly, folates are essential to reduce the risk of neural tube defects like Spina Bifida. For this reason, pregnant women in the first 12 weeks of pregnancy and those hoping to conceive are advised to take 400 micrograms of folic acid daily.

Where to find it: peas, dried fruit, fresh fruit, wholegrains including in bread, brown rice, soya beans, potatoes, porridge, peanuts, tomatoes, broccoli and green leafy vegetables and chickpeas. It is also added to some breakfast cereals.

Vitamin B12

What it's for: One of the very many B vitamins, B12 help our bodies make red blood cells and keeps the nervous system healthy. It helps our bodies use the energy in food efficiently and also to absorb folic acid properly. A lack of B12 in the diet leads to a form of anaemia called vitamin B12 deficiency anaemia.

Where to find it: dairy products; eggs, cheese and milk; fortified breakfast cereals; fortified soya yoghurts; fortified milk alternatives like soya, almond and oat milk; yeast extract.

Calcium

What it's for: This mineral is essential for creating your child's teeth and bones and for keeping them strong. It also has other functions such as helping your blood to clot normally and helping your muscles to contract when making a movement.

Where to find it: You can find calcium in all kinds of dairy products such as milk, cheese and yoghurt; however, if you choose not to eat them, you can also get it from green leafy vegetables, especially kale, plus it is found in tofu, soya beans, nuts, and bread. It is added to some fortified plant milks and luckily, it's thought to be more easily absorbed in the body from this source than in cow's milk.

More important vitamins and where to find them

Vitamin A

What it's for: keeps the skin and the lining of the body such as the nostrils healthy; makes your immune system strong; helps your vision at night.

Found in: It is found in red, green and yellow vegetables, especially carrots, spinach, sweet potatoes, red and yellow peppers; it's also in yellow fruits like mangoes, apricots and peaches and papaya.

Vitamin C

What it's for: this useful vitamin helps maintain cells and connective tissue like cartilage; it also maintains bones, blood vessels and skin. It helps the body to heal from a wound.

Found in: you can get it from the best-known source, oranges, both the whole fruit and their juice; from red and green peppers, from soft fruits such as strawberries and blackcurrants, from green vegetables like broccoli and brussels sprouts, and also from potatoes.

Vitamin D

What it's for: it helps to regulate your body's calcium and phosphate levels and keeps muscles, teeth and bones healthy. You can metabolise vitamin D in the body from sunlight, though most people can't get enough from this source alone between October and March, so may need a supplement. It is recommended to give your baby a vitamin D supplement if they are breastfed of between 8.5 am 10 mcg per day - you should do this even if you are taking vitamin D supplements yourself. If formula feeding, check if your chosen milk has a supplement already – most do. Once you start weaning, your little one should be given a baby-friendly, good quality supplement of Vitamins A, C and D. Vitamin D3 supplement is made from lichen and is suitable for vegans. This is generally presented as drops in an olive oil base.

Found in: There are few vegan sources for vitamin D, though there is some in cereals and other fortified foods like non-dairy spreads. It is recommended to give babies and children a supplement as above.

Vitamin E

What it's for: good for keeping your eyes healthy, maintaining good skin and giving your immune system a boost.

Found in: you can get this from plant oils such as sunflower, corn, soya and olive oils, in seeds, some nuts and from wheatgerm, which is found in some cereals.

Vitamin K

What it's for: if you get wounded, your blood needs to clot and vitamin K helps this process. It may also help keep your bones healthy.
Found in: spinach, broccoli and other green, leafy vegetables, some vegetables oils and in cereal grains.

Discussion: The newborn Vitamin K injection

In the UK, babies are routinely given an injection of Vitamin K soon after birth, to prevent a condition called haemorrhagic disease of the newborn (HDN), also called vitamin K deficiency bleeding (VKDB).

As all babies are born with insufficient vitamin K in their bodies, which helps the blood to clot, babies are given this shot to prevent uncontrolled bleeding from haermorrhage or injury.

It is usually injected into the baby's thigh intramuscularly and if given this way, your child only needs one dose. If you prefer to have your baby given this vitamin orally (by mouth), they will need two doses within their first week of life and one a month later, though if they vomit, you can't be sure they have received the recommended dose.

Parents became concerned about a link between Vitamin K and leukaemia several years ago due to a 1992 study that seemed to suggest a link.

Omega 3

What it's for: Omega 3 acids have a source of docosahexaenoic acid (DHA), which helps eye and brain development. It is also thought to reduce heart disease.

Found in: not many vegan sources offer Omega 3 but it can be found in lin-seeds or flaxseeds and their oil; plus walnuts, chia and hemp seeds.

Iodine

What it's for: it helps create the thyroid hormone

Found in: some vegetables, especially kelp and other seaweed, some cereals and grains.

Zinc

What it's for: this substance is good for making new enzymes and cells in the body and for healing the body too. It can help the body make use of protein, fats and carbohydrates in food.

Found in: bread and wheatgerm, often found in cereals.

Infant supplements

A vegan diet can be low in certain nutrients and so it makes sense to have a think about offering your child a good quality supplement from their early years. Look for drops or liquid that can be added to their food or a drink and later on, you can find some jelly (look for vegan versions) sweet-like vitamins in appealing shapes that your child can chew. Make sure you stick to the approved dose and never leave them where your child could reach them.

Chapter Five

How to tell others that you're bring up a plant-based baby

You have probably already come had many comments and opinions from friends and relatives when you went vegetarian or vegan – well, wait until you explain to people that you're going to be bringing your baby up the same way!

It's a fact of life that everyone, even strangers you meet in the street, feel it's fine to offer unsolicited parenting advice.

"That baby should have a hat on," they'll say, despite your having left the house with a hat and your baby pulling it off every five seconds and has now lost it. "Why doesn't he have socks on?" They will ask, forgetting the losing battle with their own children who seemed, like magicians, to be able to make socks disappear. People will have opinions about whether or not you breastfeed - and will still give you a hard time either way. One thing's for sure and you'd better learn it now – you can't win!

Ultimately, of course, it's nobody's business but yours how you bring your child up, as long as you don't make choices that could harm their health, so you would be within your rights to ignore them or tell them to mind their own business. However, that's sometimes easier said than done and you may want to reassure people that your choices are reasoned and thought-through and that your little one will be healthy and happy. You may wish to reassure family in particular that you do know what you're doing and are more aware of nutrition and where to get nutrients than most people are, because of your interest in your health and diet – and due to the tips and recipes in this book!

One way to be sure you can help others understand is to make sure you do your research thoroughly, so you are well equipped to explain to others your food choices. If you are questioned or even attacked for your beliefs by others who don't fully understand, it can be hard to justify your choices. That's why doing your research and having facts at your fingertips can help.

Try to memorise a few simple facts and some reasons for your choices. Of course, these will be a little different for each person, so do what's right for you.

The health argument

We now know, and every recently published piece of advice tells us, that eating certain foods can be bad for us. Processed meats are one of the most notorious, as there is now a proven link between their consumption and bowel cancer. A study by the World Health Organisation in 2015 said that: "small increases in the risk of several cancers may be associated with high consumption of red meat or processed meat." It defines processed meat as: "hot dogs (frankfurters), ham, sausages, corned beef, and biltong or beef jerky as well as canned meat and meat-based preparations and sauces."

Meat and fats

Animal products such as meat and dairy products also contain some things we really don't want or need too much of in our bodies. Cholesterol is one; also saturated fats and trans fats.

The NHS Live Well website tells us: "Too much saturated fat can increase the amount of cholesterol in the blood, which increases your risk of heart disease."

Though we need some fats in our diet, a modern Western diet can be high in fat, especially saturated fat (the fats found in foods like lard, butter, clarified butter or ghee, fatty meat and cheese). Too much fat can raise your cholesterol levels and that can lead to heart disease. Vegan diets are naturally low on both fats and saturated fats, so you can ensure that your diet and that of your baby will not put this strain on their developing body. However, you do need to watch out for 'hidden' fats in things like vegan cheese that may have as much fat as regular, dairy cheese. Palm oil also contains saturated fat, as does coconut oil and coconut cream. Most other saturated fats are only found in animal-derived products. Trans fats are found in hydrogenated vegetable oil, so look for and avoid that on labels too – it has to be listed as an ingredient.

Most people should try to avoid eating too much fat and to swap saturated fats for unsaturated ones and monounsaturated fats. The former are found in plant oils and the latter in olive and rapeseed oils, olive oil spread and rapeseed oil spread, avocadoes and certain nuts like peanuts, brazil nuts and almonds. You should also include some polyunsaturated fats in your diet, which are a good source of Omega-3 and Omega-6; the body can't make these and has to absorb them in the form of food. Omega-6 fats can be found in vegetable oils including sunflower, corn and rapeseed oils and also in nuts. Omega-3 fats, however, are mostly found in oily fish, so vegans have to find them in other forms such as in seeds like hemp and chia (both very good sources), seaweed, algae, walnuts, edamame beans, kidney beans and soybean oil. There are also vegan-friendly supplements you can take.

Some quick-fire statements on vegan food choices

'I prefer a vegan diet, as eating red meat and especially processed meat has been proven to cause bowel cancer.'

'I give my child a vegan diet because it's low in saturated fat, which can lead to weight gain and heart disease.'

'I get plenty of 'good' fats from nuts, seeds and avocado.'

The animal cruelty argument

Many of us are inspired to become vegan to avoid animal cruelty and this can be a pretty powerful argument. Unfortunately, it's also one many people find deeply disturbing, so choose how you share information about how animals are treated for the mainstream meat and dairy industry, when talking to friends and family who eat them, as it can actively put people off listening if they feel too challenged – and let's face it, if they knew and understood the full horrors of what happens to some animals, they wouldn't want to eat a sausage ever again. Better to inspire by example than to preach.

Being attacked for your beliefs

Sadly, some people feel that vegans are fair game for humour, a bit of 'banter' or a downright attack. The attacks tend to come in one of three forms; here's how to counter them.

How to counter the aggressive attack: "But I bet you wear leather."

This is something that always gets said to vegans and vegetarians. Even if you do wear some leather (or have the odd item made of silk or a piano with ivory keys), choosing not to eat animal products means that you are already actively making a difference not just to your own health but also to the amount of meat that needs to be produced in this country. You're already making a difference. If you do choose to go the next step to avoid animal products in your clothes and household products, there are lots of fantastic vegan-friendly clothing, shoe and home wares companies to look at.

How to counter the mock-empathy argument: "I don't eat much meat, only chicken."

Actually, you could argue that chicken is one of the worst things to eat, if that's all you eat. If it's a battery chicken from a supermarket, it has probably had a miserable life, will have been pumped full of hormones and water and be nutritionally negligible. If you hear this statement, you could perhaps gently suggest that the person speaking try to ensure their meat is free-range, cruelty free and raised ethically.

How to answer the fake veggie: "I'm practically vegan. I only eat fish and dairy."

Many people have very poor grasp of what is an animal product and what isn't. It would seem simple to most of us that, if the source the food comes from has a face, it's an animal product. But not everyone has such easy understanding of the facts. I once asked for sample menus for a conference I was organising and had to ring to say I hadn't received the vegetarian choice. The person organising the catering told me I already had it, and it was the chicken. I told her that vegetarians didn't eat chicken to which she replied: "Yes they do – I'm vegetarian and I eat chicken." Others tell me they are "pescatarian" or "flexitarian" which is basically just a way of saying they eat what they like but give it what they perceive to be a trendy name! Try to help people understand where their food comes from and what would constitute a more ethical or sustainable source.

What if it were a religion?

What really annoys me is that when I am challenged or someone makes a joke about vegans, how disrespectful they are of my ethics. If I were Jewish or Muslim and refused pork, or Hindu and refused beef, or any other religion that has dietary laws, my views would be respected. Why is a religion more acceptable to some that ethics? This is an interesting problem that I'm not sure we know the answer to.

How to answer the questions most people just can't wait to ask you.

"Where do you get your iron / protein / calcium?"

You can turn back to chapter three to find out where the protein comes from, and as you create delicious meals for your baby, you can point them out to your friends and family. "Tonight, we're giving baby lentil balls and rainbow veg. That contains calcium, iron, protein and lots of vitamins and we're also giving her a supplement containing the B12 and vitamins A, C and D." You can also turn the argument back around on the person questioning you. "So, what did you have for dinner last night? Where do you get your anti-oxidants? What vitamins were in the meal you had? Aren't you concerned about your lack of B12 and fibre?" Many people who have what they think of as a 'normal' diet would not be able to answer when questioned about specific nutrients. Chances are that if they have to feel they need to know the nutritional content of every meal they've had recently when they meet you, they will stop asking about yours.

"We're omnivores, that's why we have both incisors and molars, so we must be designed to eat both animal products and vegetables, yes?"

Well, yes, humans have evolved with teeth that allow them to eat both meat and fish plus fruit and vegetables. But we, unlike animals, have free choice. We can choose what we eat, and we have the intellect to make sure we get all we need from our chosen diet.

"Our bodies are designed to need some animal products"

Actually, many people have proved that a diet based mostly on vegetables and fruit can be completely nutritious. The population of Southern India are largely vegetarian and if you examine the populations of some of the world's most long-lived populations, such as those in Japan and the Mediterranean, you'll find that their diet has a carbohydrate like rice, plus they have lots of vegetables and small amounts of meat or fish and then not every day. As long as you have the essential ingredients in your vegan diet, you and your baby will be fine.

"Don't you eat 'normal' food? Is it all raw vegetables?"

You can point out to friends how much of what they think of as 'normal' food is actually vegan already. They tend to think of us as eating weird, complex meals made entirely of quinoa and tofu, with perhaps some sprouting beans for good measure. Actually, that sounds delicious. Talk to them instead about pasta with vegetable-based sauces (not fresh pasta as that's often made with egg), rice, potatoes, pizza (choose this with no cheese or with vegan cheese), chips, veggie sausage and mash, veggie Shepherds' Pie and so on. Tell them about the normal sounding meals and how great that vegan burger was at the street market or festival. Also, point out how, when you're on a plane and the veggies get served first, everyone wants what they have.

"How can you get enough iron?"

You can say: "My baby's meal tonight contains spinach, tofu and lentils, which all contain iron."

"Won't you make your child sick? Isn't it a form of child abuse?

Some people say that you shouldn't force your beliefs on your child when they aren't old enough to make the choice – but don't we do that for everything we choose for our children? We choose what immunisations we give them, what to dress them in, whether to strap them into a car seat and drive them around, what nursery they should go to, what education they should have – so why shouldn't you decide on their diet too? As long as your child is well and happy – and you should make sure you keep all your appointments with your doctor and health visitor to ensure they are putting on weight and growing properly – then you know you're doing a good job.

I have had people ask: "What happens if he / she wants to go to McDonald's with his / her friends?" This was one that actually stumped me. Can you imagine saying to an Orthodox Jew that their child might 'one day want' to have a bacon sandwich to be 'more like their friends?' Try asking them to turn the sentence around to include another minority group and see if they think it still sounds acceptable.

"I went vegetarian / vegan but my doctor told me I shouldn't do it" / or the greatest one of all time, "I went vegetarian but I really fancied a bacon sandwich, so I stopped."

It's a very British trait that we are a bit of an all-or-nothing country. Started a diet and then eaten a cake? The diet's off. Became a vegan? Really craved a sausage - so went back to eating meat. People don't seem to consider that they could eat the cake or the sausage, then go back to the diet or vegan lifestyle. If your motives are for better health or for animal welfare, then surely anything you do helps a bit? Don't be downhearted if you need to eat something slightly outside your preferred diet once in a while if that's all there is on offer – for example, if all I have had to eat is a cheese sandwich with no vegan alternative, I was still doing better for myself and the planet if I did this. Then you eat a vegan diet again. If you really wouldn't countenance eating diary once you've gone vegan, just make sure you plan ahead and take food for you and your little one when you go out.

"I eat free-range meat. The animal has a great life and is killed painlessly."

Thinking that an animal is happy and healthy, frolicking in the fields and running through the forests, makes it even sadder that you feel it's OK to kill that animal just so you can have a steak or a chop. Isn't it? You may want to explore just how 'natural' the lives of farm animals, even free-range ones, are and talk to your friends about that.

"Vegans think they're better than everyone else. You're so smug."

This is a frequent attack. Why does our lifestyle choice invoke such a strong reaction? Mostly, I suspect, because deep down, many people know that it's ethically unsustainable to continue with meat production the way it is right now and they know it's damaging the planet, too. They feel that we are challenging them and judging them. If that makes them think about their options, fine but many people will clam up and refuse to listen to reason. Mind you, I think the person who sums it up best is comedian Romesh Ranganathan.

"People hate vegans and the reason they hate vegans is because they think we're humorless, they think we think we're better than non-vegans, they think we're always banging on about it, and all of those things are true. I am better than you if you're not vegan. In terms of my ethical decisions, I am so much better than you. I'm better for the planet, I'm better for the animals. There's nothing worse about me apart from I'm slightly irritating to have round for dinner."

Romesh revealed that he had a very strong reaction to this statement and that his social media was taken over for several weeks by, on the one hand, vegans telling him he's great and on the other, meat eaters attacking him. It does evoke strong reactions – we need to embrace that rather than being afraid to speak up.

"Being vegan is so difficult and it's really expensive to eat organic."

If you can cook, you can cook vegan. If you're a good cook, you can whip up meals that even the most die-hard omnivore will wolf down. I once served my meat-eating father a dish of cauliflower cheese. After three helpings, I told him it was vegan. "No it isn't." he said.

Organic vegetables and fruit may be slightly more expensive than 'mainstream' ones – but I think it's worth the extra money not to put pesticides and chemical fertilisers into my baby.

"I would miss bacon / steak / chicken too much."

It's a very funny thing but the less you have of something, the less you want it. I found that I was eating less and less dairy about eight years ago and then finally made the switch to a vegan lifestyle after a Christmas when I over-indulged in cheese and creamy desserts. I just didn't want them anymore.

You may find this is true for you. If not and you want to eat vegan, there are some great meat alternatives now and you can make some convincing meat substitutes into things like duck pancakes and BLTs.

"Plants feel pain too."

Ah, the last refuge of the cynic. Plants don't have a central nervous system. End of. Or you could say: "I tell you what, I have two ideas for a day out with the kids – shall we go and pick strawberries or visit the abattoir?"

Chapter Six

Spoon fed or baby-led? Plus, what you'll need.

Baby-led weaning: the benefits

- Babies love to imitate, so if they see you eating, using your hands or using cutlery, they love to do the same. This will help them get to a stage where they can feed themselves more easily.
- If you have older children, they can all eat the same thing at the same time. This will save you time, as you don't have to mash or purée the food.
- Babies love to grab things. If you offer them soft food that comes in a fist-sized piece, they will enjoy being in charge of when and how it goes in their mouth. The fine motor skills of the pincer grip, when you bring the thumb and finger tips together, comes later.
- Babies who are offered all sorts of food to try for themselves may be able to cope better with different textures from an earlier age. They may also be able to make healthier choices – though you do have to offer healthy food in the first place!

And the downside? It's messy! Invest in a large washable mat or use a picnic blanket if you don't have an easy to clean kitchen floor.

Safety note: avoid baby-led weaning if your child has any developmental problems that might make chewing or swallowing difficult and if your baby was born prematurely, make sure you again follow the signs that your baby is ready to wean. This may be when they reach their due date plus six months, rather than six months after birth.

Spoon-fed weaning: the benefits

- You can keep track of what and how much your baby is eating far more easily if you are spooning the food into their mouth.
- You can ensure your baby is getting sufficient quantities of the protein and vegetable or fruit element of a meal if you're in charge, especially if it is mixed together in a purée.
- Your baby may get frustrated if they have to feed themselves, especially if they are tired or are dropping a lot of it.
- It's much less messy than baby-led weaning.
- There is less chance of your baby choking when you start with smooth purées.

And the downside? It can be time-consuming mashing up tiny quantities of food for your baby's meals and you may find you cook different things than you are making for the rest of the family. If you use special equipment, it also adds to the washing up bowl.

Note on both spoon fed and baby-led: lumpy food helps with your baby's development and it is very important that babies be given food with lumps in, or pieces of food to eat themselves, by the time they are 10 months. If this doesn't happen, it can be hard to get the child to accept food with texture or lumps. Eating lumps also helps with the development of the mouth and helps with talking.

Safety note: Pay attention to the signs that your baby is ready to begin weaning on page 14 and make sure you supervise your child at all times when they are eating, to avoid choking risks.

Equipment – what you'll need and what's handy to have

You need surprisingly little for weaning your baby, though many of us end up with drawers and cupboards full of gear. Buy little and as you need it and try not to believe you have to have every gadget going – though a few judiciously purchased bits of gear can make your life so much easier! Here are some ideas of what is great to have and what's nice if you can afford (and have room to store) it.

What baby sits in

A good highchair is really helpful for weaning, as it is the right height to have your baby sitting at the table with you, which helps them feel part of family meals. Try to look for one that will grow with your baby and that can be used for many years (or if you do buy one that's just for babies, make sure you pass it on to another parent when you have finished using it). Wooden highchairs are far more sustainable than those made from plastic and there are several chairs that turn into adult chairs later on, so you won't waste money on something that's only used for a short time.

You could also use a baby bouncing seat to feed your baby, as long as it has a good sitting-up position, with you sitting on the floor in front of your baby. Never place a baby seat on top of a table, as your baby could fall off.

When you're out, you can feed your baby in the pushchair – some have seats that raise up to a higher position so that your baby can be pulled up to the table. Alternatively, you could look for a travel highchair. From simple fabrics options that tie onto a chair to more complex ones that clip to the table, there are several around. This helps you and your baby get out and about.

Plates and bowls

You could use your normal bowls and plates for your baby - but of course there's the possibility that the baby will swipe them off the highchair tray, causing breakages. You may want to buy some special non-breakable bowls and small plates. Look for sustainable options such as bamboo, or if you do end up with plastic, make sure you pass them on to another mum when you finish with them. You need a couple of each ideally, so one might be in the dish washer while you use the other.

You can also buy bowls with sealable lids, great for taking food with you when you're out and about with baby. Snack pots are great too and avoid you having to buy small packets of snacks when you're out, leading to more packaging waste. Some pots can be used to store the food in the fridge or freezer and also for re-heating and taking out with you.

Note: avoid BPA

Remember to look for plastic containers that say they are BPA free. BPA is short for Bisphenol A, a chemical that has been used in plastics and for the lining of cans and which has been shown to leach into food or liquids contained in bottles and containers. The chemical is thought to have an adverse effect on our bodies and now most items for babies are BPA-free..

Cutlery

Small spoons are ideal for feeding your baby and though you could use a simple teaspoon, a softer spoon feels less harsh on your little one's delicate lips and tongue. You can buy silicone spoons or packs of little colourful plastic versions. You can even find bamboo options. If you're looking for spoons for you to feed your baby with, they can be very simple. However, if your baby is being offered one to try out baby-led weaning, there are some great shapes that are easier for babies to grasp themselves. Some have angled handles, others wider handles with holes for little fingers and silicone areas to help them hold on even when the spoon is covered with food.

You can also buy little baby-sized sets of knives, forks and spoons. Again, some have angled or easy to grip handles and are just the right size for little fists. They also make lovely keepsakes for your child.

Baby food processor

There are plenty of labour-saving devices if you want to treat yourself and actually, they can be used for other purposes too if you're a keen cook; for coulis and sauces and for making small quantities of chopped herbs or similar.

From a simple mini hand blender to gadgets that cook, steam and then blend your baby's food, there are plenty of items available that can help you to make great and delicious baby food. If you like batch cooking, you can use a larger processor or one with two chambers so that you can make more food at once.

Look for items that are easy to clean, that fit with the way you like to cook and that suit your lifestyle.

Drinking cup

Your baby should be encouraged to drink from a cup or beaker from about six months, when you start to wean and you should stop using a bottle completely by around one year. Look for a cup that your baby can grasp with both hands. There are all sorts out there, from ones that are difficult to knock over to angled cups that make drinking easier. Offer water with meals.

Weaning pots for storing and feeding with lids

If you like to plan well ahead, look for pots that you can store the food you make for your baby in the fridge and freezer. Avoid buying too many of the versions that are very small, as your baby will soon be eating more at each meal. You can use ice cube trays when your baby is first starting to try those first flavours.

Freezer bags

When you have made and frozen some food, you can pop the frozen cubes out and store them in a freezer bag. Look for eco-friendly, reusable ones.

Bibs

Keeping food off your baby's clothes is a must, so look for a batch of bibs that you can wash or wipe clean. Some have sleeves, which helps with baby-led weaning. You should also invest in some dribble bibs, which will save you having to change your baby's top often when they are teething.

Cooler bag

Taking a meal or two out with you? A small cooler bag is a great addition to your cooking equipment and can be packed under the pushchair.

Many baby changing bags come with a sleeve that keeps drinks cool or warm too.

Splash mat / plastic sheet / washable mat

If you have a non-washable kitchen or dining room floor, such as carpet, you'll need something to protect it. This can be as simple as a decorator's plastic sheet or you could use a baby brand washable cloth with plastic backing, a bit like a picnic blanket.

Do I need to sterilise my baby's feeding equipment?

Once your baby reaches six months, you don't need to sterilise their feeding bowls, spoons and accessories but do make sure they have been washed well in hot, soapy water or in a dishwasher, then left to dry thoroughly.

However, you should sterilise objects that come into contact with breast or formula milk. You should sterilise any equipment used for feeding your baby breast or formula milk under six months but remember not to start weaning until this age has been reached.

Chapter Seven

The early days: introducing different foods to your baby, leading into Stage One

The first thing to say is - relax!

Weaning does not mean that you should aim to have your baby on three meals a day within a few days.

Starting from six months, you should simply aim to introduce new foods to your baby gently and slowly. It's very much a 'suck it and see' attitude – literally!

Blander and more gently flavoured foods are usually considered the best things to start off with and as your baby gets used to flavours, you can start to introduce stronger ones, though your baby might surprise you by liking a strong flavour straight away.

Texture is also very important, and you should start off with fruit, vegetables, proteins and pulses that have easy to mash textures – not very fibrous foods.

Also, don't worry about whether you consider something suitable for a particular time of day – babies aren't at all bothered if they have peas for breakfast or cereal for lunch.

It's much better to offer foods at times when your baby is alert and responsive and when it's a good time for you, too.

Safety note about potential allergies: After each new food, make sure you watch your baby to note any adverse reactions.

Remember that you may need to introduce a new food to your baby seven times or even more before they accept it - don't give up after a couple of tries!

If it has been a while since you gave your baby a particular food, it will count as a new flavour when you cook it again, especially with produce that's very seasonal.

Be a good role model.

Remember that babies are very imitative and like to copy you, so make sure you and the rest of the family are eating the food you offer your baby. It's not good trying to feed your little one their greens if you are eating chips!

The first flavours

Baby rice

This has been one of the most popular weaning foods for generations and no wonder – it's gluten and allergen free, is filling and can be mixed with your breastmilk or your baby's usual milk to make it taste familiar.

It can be found in the shops with added iron, calcium and vitamins, so check the packets - and also look for organic versions.

For those first few feeds, mix one teaspoon of rice with a tablespoon of baby's usual milk – preferably expressed breastmilk, at body temperature.

As your baby gets used to the taste and texture, you can then make it to a thicker consistency.

It's ideal as a feed in the evening, just before a warm bath and followed by a sleepy-time breastfeed. It's also excellent for breakfast, too.

Many baby rice products that come in a packet have added vitamin B1 (thiamine), which helps the body break down and release the energy from food and is also a good nutritional boost for the nervous system.

This is not stored by the body, so we need a source every day.

Never be tempted to add rice to your baby's milk due to the risk of choking or inhalation.

Porridge

Suitable form six months, this is a fabulous grain for your baby's diet and has no known allergens.

This can be made and served in exactly the same way as rice, above. Use finely ground oats.

Tip: You can add any of the fruits on the next page to baby rice or porridge – choose a single fruit purée, then add a second and maybe a third.

Keep mixing it up to avoid food boredom! You'll find a handy chart of some great flavour combinations a bit further on.

Single, raw fruit purées – uncooked fruits and soft baby-led foods

Softer fruits can be simply peeled, stones or pips removed and then mashed or blended. If you think there might be some tough or stringy parts or small pips, you can also sieve the fruit – this purées the fruit very finely! Softer pieces of fruit can be cut into baby's fist-sized pieces and offered to chew on.

Banana; mash and add to baby rice, offer short chunks for baby to feed herself

Peach, nectarine and apricot; very ripe fruits can be mashed finely with a fork or blended. Chunks can be chewed on by your baby.

Strawberry; Can be puréed, mashed or cut into small chunks. Some babies have a slight reaction to these, so keep an eye on your baby.

Raspberry; because this has tiny seeds, it's best sieved and can be served as a sauce on baby rice or porridge. Halved fruits can be offered to your baby but make sure you keep an eye on them to avoid a choke hazard.

Kiwi fruit; scoop out the seeds and mash the flesh. Whole pieces of the green part of the fruit can be held and chewed.

Pineapple; purée in a blender. Beware that some people are allergic to pineapple. Try to pick out any fibrous pieces.

Avocados; great as a finger food or offer mashed or puréed.

Melon and watermelon; great as finger foods and the colours look appealing to your little one too.

Cherry; remove the stone first, pass through a sieve to remove the skins or blend to make a sauce.

Mango and Papaya; mash or blend, adding a little water if needed. Soft sticks can be offered as a finger food.

Blueberries, redcurrants, blackcurrants; chop up for baby-led weaning or blend to make a sauce for yoghurt, baby rice or porridge.

Citrus fruits; babies can chew on chunks of oranges, tangerines, satsumas and grapefruit from six months but make sure you are very careful to remove all pips, membranes and skin from the segments before offering them. They can also be added into other fruit mixtures and their juice used too. Some babies have a slight reaction to citrus fruits which can cause them to have more nappy rash. If this is the case, avoid for a while and try to re-introduce later on.

Cooked fruit purées

Try these purées on their own, mixed with another fruit, or served over rice or porridge. Most of these fruits can be peeled or stoned where necessary, cut into small chunks, cooked with a little water and then mashed or blended. You can also cook any of the softer fruit previously listed (above) and use on their own or mixed with other, firmer fruits.

Apple, pear and quince – peel, core and cube, then gently steam, and purée. Add a few drops of lemon juice both for flavour and to help avoid the fruit going brown.

Rhubarb – remove stringy outer edges, cut into chunks and boil in a little water. Mash well or blend.

Dried fruits such as figs and raisins are great too – make sure you remove any tough, stringy parts after you have cooked them and add them to other fruit mixes.

Two and three fruit purées

Try these flavour combinations

Two fruit combinations

Banana and peach
Strawberry and apple
Mango and pear
Banana and fig
Apple and raisin
Apple and pear
Mango and apple
Banana and blueberry
Apple and apricot
Cherry and apple
Blueberry and nectarine
Rhubarb and apple

Three fruit combinations

Watermelon, pear and fig
Banana, apple and raisin
Cherry, strawberry and banana
Mango, apple and peach
Pear, quince and fig
Raspberry, apple and apricot
Blueberry, banana and raisin
Cherry, redcurrant and blueberry
Nectarine, peach and pear
Avocado, banana and apple
Apricot, pear and mango
Kiwi fruit, apple and banana

Experiment with more flavours and see what you come up with! Don't forget to add spices such as cinnamon, nutmeg, allspice and more but go easy!

Cooked vegetables

Tomatoes – one of the most versatile of all veg (yes, we know it's a fruit), it can be offered raw or cooked. It's probably most useful as an ingredient or sauce, so look for our simple tomato sauce recipe on page 100 and for ideas for including it in meals in the recipe pages.

Carrots - raw as sticks, these are great for scooping up yummy hummus, cooked as a finger food or mashed or puréed.

Courgette – cute into fist-size chunks. Use a small amount of water plus a teaspoon of vegan butter substitute and choose a pot with a tight lid, Allow the water and butter mixture to come to a gentle boil, then steam in the juices for a few minutes. Offer a few chunks to your baby to eat (remove skin from these pieces and the outsides, not the inner part where the seeds are, are best) and mash the remainder. You can also use this technique with fennel and marrow.

Fennel – see above or steam and mash.

Sweetcorn – boil for a few minutes, then use a blender to make a smooth paste. Make sure to remove tough fibres, especially if you are using fresh corn on the cob. It should be cooked and puréed until your baby has teeth and can chew the kernels. There is some evidence that some babies can have an allergic reaction to sweetcorn.

Green beans, Bobby beans and runner beans - remove fibrous side threads, seeds and the stalk end. Steam or boil, then offer whole beans for your baby to chew on or mash or blend in purées.

Spinach, sorrel and watercress – packed with iron, these can be steamed very lightly and blended.

Swede, parsnips, turnips, beetroot, celeriac, Jerusalem artichoke, potato – these should be peeled and chopped into chunks, then cooked in a little water or steamed. They can then be mashed or puréed or offered as fist-sized chunks.

Pumpkin, yam and squash – peel, remove all seeds and stringy inner parts and cook in water or steam. Soft chunks can be offered as finger food.

Asparagus – cook or steam and offer mashed or as whole spears to chew on.

Pak Choi – steam and then blend with a little water. When your child can chew, offer the firmer stems as a finger food and the green leaves as a shredded vegetable or purée.

Broccoli and Romanesco – one of the best finger foods ever, babies will love chewing on these 'baby trees,' or they can be used mashed and mixed with other vegetables.

Cauliflower – use in a similar way to broccoli, though it may need cooking slightly longer.

Brussels Sprouts – steam and mash or cut into slices and drizzle with a little melted vegetable spread or olive oil.

Cabbage and Spring Greens, Chard, Cavolo Nero, endives, Kale – steam or oil, then blend or serve finely shredded once baby can chew.

Peppers – grill these with the skin up, then the skin can be peeled off when it cools. Mash or blend the flesh.

Broad beans, peas – if frozen, bring to the boil and then drain, blend or mash. Broad beans can have slightly tough skins, so you can remove them if you have the patience! Best bought fresh when in season, pod them first.

Runner beans – cut off the ends and remove stringy edges if any, can be offered whole to chew on, puréed or mashed.

Aubergine – peel and remove any seeds (though most don't have them if they're quite small). They can be roasted, boiled, steamed, fried or microwaved. They can also be given as bite-size chunks.

Onions, spring onions, leeks and garlic – use these for flavour. They can be sautéed and then added to vegetables before they are blended.

Artichokes, globe – steam for an hour, remove the leaves and scoop the edible flesh from the bottom. Remove the choke (the hairy bit), mash up the heart too.

Artichokes, Jerusalem – treat these like potatoes but do be aware that they can cause wind, so if your baby is a sufferer, it may be best to avoid.

Mushrooms – best cooked as some can have bacteria on them. Fry gently or steam and add to other vegetable blends.

Spinach – wash thoroughly and steam, then blend.

Potatoes and sweet potatoes – peel, cube and boil or steam. Can be offered as chunks or mashed. Great mixed with other vegetables.

Raw vegetables

Some vegetables are best eaten raw because they're great that way – and others are best raw to preserve their nutrients. Once your little one can chew and has a good number of teeth, these can be cut into little sticks and eaten alone or with a delicious dip.

Cucumber	Tomato	Radish
Watercress	Pak Choi	Cabbage and Kale
Lettuce	Chicory	Endive and Rocket

Pulses and legumes

If you are using dried pulses or legumes, you need to pay attention to how you cook them – you can find out from the packet instructions, so make sure you check that out. Some need to be soaked overnight, then boiled. Others, like small lentils, can be cooked from their dry state.

The benefit of cooking beans and pulses yourself from dried for baby food is two-fold; firstly, it's cheaper, as you can buy dried beans very inexpensively and

secondly, many tins of beans have brine inside to preserve the beans. This can be quite high in salt and you shouldn't add salt to your baby's food, so you need to bear this in mind when buying. If you do buy in cans, wash them well or look for low sodium options. If you're soaking and cooking beans, you could make a meal for the whole family like a nice bean stew or chilli rather than trying to cook a tiny amount for your baby's meal.

Mixing it up - using two or three vegetable and legume purée flavours together

Two vegetable combinations

Spinach and peas
Pea and mint
Spinach and potatoes
Chard and spring onions
Peppers and tomato
Leek and potato
Butternut squash and carrot
Lentil and carrot
Cauliflower and asparagus
Butternut squash and tomato
Artichoke and red peppers
Broad beans and spinach
Sweet potato and squash
Carrot and broad bean
Sweet potatoes and courgette
Green bean and avocado
Broccoli and Cannelini beans
Cannelini beans and carrot
Split peas and squash
Cabbage and butterbean

Three vegetable combinations

Spinach, potatoes and peas
Pea, carrot and mint
Chard, lentil and carrot
Butternut squash, lentil and tomato
Artichoke, spinach and courgette
Red peppers, broad beans and carrot
Squash, broad bean and tomato
Spinach, butterbean and courgette
Carrot, squash and black beans
Chard, peppers and potatoes
Carrot, artichoke and pea
Cabbage, sweetcorn, spring onion
Leek, pea and kidney bean
Split peas, squash and parsnip
Parsnips, lentils and pea
Broccoli, parsnip and beetroot
Pumpkin, kale and green beans
Courgette, red pepper and onion
Kidney bean, carrot and sweet potato
Watercress, kale and potato

Fist friendly foods for Baby-Led Weaning

Whether you want to try spoon fed or baby-led weaning, or a combination of the two, you can offer all of the above fruits, vegetables, pulses and legumes to your baby in fist-sized chunks.

Why not offer your baby a few pieces of baby-led weaning foods while you offer some spoons of food? This allows them some independence and you can alternate a couple of spoonsful of purée with some snacks they feed themselves. Any food that is soft enough to eat raw, as above, can be cut into chunky chip size – about the right size for your baby to grasp in a fist.

Remember to avoid offering food that could cause choking, so anything that's roughly grape sized is out of bounds. Grapes themselves should always be cut into halves or quarters to avoid the risk of choking.

Chapter Eight

The recipes

Once you have got beyond the single or double purée stage, here are some tasty and nutritious meals that give your baby a good range of all the vitamins, minerals and protein they need.

How to use these recipes: Each recipe has options for additional stages, so you might have a smooth purée for Stage One, lumps for Stage Two and leave the food whole for Stage Three. Many also have options of how to use the recipe for the whole family, so a purée might easily be turned into a soup and a stew or aburger suggestion might make a great option for all. I'm passionate about the whole family taking time to sit down around the table, eating properly whilst still remaining true to your ethics of eating a plant based diet, so I hope this makes it easier. Continue milk feeds as usual. There are also tips for most meals if you'd like to use the Baby-Led Weaning approach or a mixture of spoon-fed and baby-led. In addition, although most of these recipes are vegan, there are some suggestions for how to include a vegetarian option.

All measurements are given in cups, grams and millilitres, so it's easy no matter what measuring devices you have. A set of cup measures is very handy – see our equipment list on page 41. Oven temperatures are in Celius.

Timeline - what they eat and when

From six months; the first couple of weeks, you will be offering single fruit or vegetable tastes once a day. It may be just a couple of spoons or bites. Watch for reactions. After a couple of weeks, introduce new flavours.

From seven months; start to mix a couple of ingredients together and continue to introduce new flavours. Offer baby-led snacks too.

From eight months; start to introduce texture by leaving some foods chunky and by offering soft foods for your baby to feed themself. Have a couple of meal times and a snack a day at this stage. Mix two or three flavours together, keep exploring.

From nine months; as your baby's appetite increases, add a third meal. Keep trying new textures and flavours and mix two or three together. Try some simple recipes.

From ten months; your baby may now eat three meals and maybe a snack too. Your little one may become less interested in milk now.

From eleven to twelve months; your baby may be keen to feed himself and is getting better at using a cup.

From twelve months - congratulations! you've given your baby a great start in life!

Breakfast

Baby Bircher

Make this yummy breakfast the evening before and pop it in the fridge overnight, so you'll have a delicious meal to wake up to.

Ingredients

One and a half cups (60g) finely ground porridge oats
1 fresh, crunchy apple; Braeburn or Pink Lady apples are great
¼ tsp cinnamon
Oat milk to cover

What to do

Finely grate the apple, skin and all, then mix it with the oats and oat milk. Add the cinnamon to taste and then cover the bowl, leaving it in the fridge overnight to allow the flavours to mingle together and the oats to soften.

Mix it up

Experiment with different fruits so that you and your baby don't get bored. Try peaches and apricots, soft fruits such as strawberries, raspberries and blueberries, bananas and whatever else is fresh and in season.

Stage One blend baby's portion in a mini food processor to make it smooth (may need to add a little extra milk)
Stage Two leave slightly larger pieces of fruit
Stage Three your baby is ready to eat the same version as you

Baby-Led Tip

Offer some cooled cooked apple sticks as a finger food, halved blueberries, pieces of peeled apricot or banana pieces.

Make this for the whole family

Porridge Gets Fruity

Make a simple bowl of filling porridge and then experiment with different fruits that are in season.

Ingredients

½ cup finely ground porridge oats
One cup oat or breast milk
Fruit of your choice, such as raspberries, strawberries, blueberries.

See page 51 for more two and three fruit purée ideas .

What to do

Make the baby porridge with finely ground oats (remember, no cow's milk under one year). Blend some of the fruit with the porridge. Place in the bowl and top with some small
pieces of the fruits to decorate.
Use different fruits every few times you make it.
Add cinnamon or nutmeg if liked.

Mix it up

Add some extra protein with chia seeds, smooth nut butters (avoid if you suspect an allergy) or mixed seeds, all finely ground.

Warming Cinnamon Porridge

Another version of a classic oaty breakfast, this time with a spice that warms your little one's tiny tummy.

Ingredients

¼ cup (10g) of finely ground oats
A cup (230ml) of oat milk
¼ tsp ground cinnamon
Half a banana

What to do

Soak the oats for half an hour in the oat milk, then gently heat on top of the stove and stir until cooked through. Add the mashed banana and cinnamon.

Tip

This meal works for all baby weaning stages and for adults too, though make sure the oats are very fine for Stage One.

Baby Oats with Pear Purée

Oatmeal is such a filling breakfast that it makes a great choice for energetic little ones. Here's another option using cooked fruit.

Ingredients

Half cup (20 g) fine oats
Three quarters of a cup (180ml) of oat milk
1 ripe organic pear or apple

What to do

Mix the oats and milk together and bring to a gentle simmer. Stir and keep cooking for 5 minutes. Meanwhile, peel and core the pear and cut into baby fist-sized chunks – you'll keep some for a baby-led weaning snack. Steam the chunks until tender, then blend with a little of the cooking water. Either serve the purée mixed into the oats, or as a topping, or swirled through it. This helps your baby get used to different flavours and textures. Offer the cooled chunks at the same time so that your baby can feed herself, or later in the day, as a healthy snack.

Baby-Led Tip

Offer small pieces of the fruit as you spoon the oats into your baby's mouth. As they get older, give a spoon to your baby so she can start to feed herself.

This simple porridge can be made with a wide variety of fruit purées.

Chia with Blueberries

Packed with protein and Omega 3, chia is highly nutritious.

Ingredients

2 tsp chia seeds
2 tbsp breast milk, formula or oat milk
A handful of blueberries

What to do

Pop a couple of teaspoons of chia seeds in a bowl, cover with breast or plant milk and leave to soak for a few hours. Then add the puréed blueberries and mix well.

Stage One blend baby's portion to make it smooth
Stage Two chop the fruit finely rather than blending
Stage Three leave some larger pieces

Baby-Led Tip

Offer some sticks of soft fruit such as banana and peach or some of the blueberries, halved, between spoonfuls full of this tasty and nutritious pudding.

Layered Chia Pudding

This makes an attractive breakfast and is a development of the recipe on the left, that you can serve with different ingredients to keep little taste buds interested. Why not add a layer of vegan yoghurt too? Don't serve in a glass, this is just for show!

Ingredients

2 tsp chia seeds
2 tbsp breast or plant milk
A handful of raspberries, blended to a purée
A desert spoon of home-made granola, finely ground (see page 69)

What to do

Cover a couple of teaspoons of chia seeds with breast or plant milk and soak for a few hours. Place a spoonful of granola at the bottom, top with some fruit purée, then some of the chia, followed by a little more granola.

Stage One finely blend the granola
Stage Two chop the fruit and crumble the granola
Stage Three leave some larger pieces of fruit and granola

Yummy Granola Bars

These nutritious little bars are great as an on-the-go snack. Make a batch and keep them in a tin for 'hangry' emergencies!

Ingredients

1 ½ cups rolled oats
¼ cup home made apple sauce (page 72)
3 tbsp cashew nut butter
½ cup mixed organic seeds (inc pumpkin, sesame, linseed etc)
¼ cup rapeseed oil
2 tbsp golden sultanas
2 tbsp dried apricots, chopped finely
½ tsp cinnamon
¼ tsp nutmeg

What to do

Put all the dry ingredients into a large bowl, add the fruit and seeds. Mix together the apple sauce and the oil, then add to the dry ingredients and mix really well until everything is combined. Spead out onto an oiled baking tray and bake at 200^0 for 30-40 minutes. While still warm, cut into little bars or squares that will just fit neatly into your little one's hand.

Stage One blend the dry ingredients and fruit before adding to make a much finer texture in the bars
Stage Two chop the seeds and fruit finely
Stage Three make chunkier bars with whole seeds and raisins

Baby-Led Tip

These are are great for your baby to feed himself, as they can be held in a little hand and chomped on. They also make a great dipper, which can be used to dip into a fruit sauce or yoghurt.

Mix it up

Try out different dried fruit or finely chopped nuts such as pistachios.

Mini Tofulettes

There's nothing nicer for a lazy brunch, between meals snack or tea time treat than a golden mini 'omelette' made with tofu, not egg.

Ingredients

1 small onion, chopped
200g tofu
A couple of tbsp of vegetables: peas, sweetcorn, finely diced peppers, tomatoes, cooked potatoes, mushrooms or any vegetables you have around
3 tbsp nutritional yeast
2 tbsp rapeseed oil
½ tsp turmeric
½ tsp vegetable bouillon
¼ tsp black pepper
3 tbsp wholemeal flour
1 tbsp cornflour
½ cup oat milk

What to do

Sauté the finely chopped onion in a little oil. Put the chopped tofu and the oat milk into a blender and pulse until it's smooth. Add the nutritional yeast and vegetable bouillon to the liquid, plus the pepper, turmeric and flour and blend again. Oil some muffin tins and place a few pieces of the mixed vegetables and onions into the tins, then pour the tofu mixture into each. Bake in the oven for 10-15 minutes at 200^{0} or until the tofu mixture is set; if it is still a little wet, turn the oven down to 160^{0} and leave it another 10 minutes. Serve hot or cold.

Stage One chop the tofulettes into small fist-sized chunks
Stage Two continue to offer small pieces
Stage Three your baby can hold a whole one and eat it

Baby-Led Tip

These are great for baby-led weaning right from the early stages. Try out different vegetables each time you make this. Add some green herbs and a kiss of garlic too!

Baby Buckwheat Pancakes

These tasty little pancakes are made with buckwheat, which is not only gluten-free but is packed with minerals and antioxidants too. It may help control blood sugar levels and is high in fibre. Make a batch of these for breakfast or they're a great snack for trips to the park.

Ingredients

1 cup buckwheat flour
2 tsp baking powder
1 cup oat milk
2 tsp apple cider vinegar or lemon juice
1 tbsp maple syrup
1 tsp vanilla essence
1 tbsp apple sauce (see recipe page 72)
½ tsp cinnamon

What to do

Mix together the dry ingredients and in another bowl, the wet ones. Stir gently until all the flour is combined with the liquid and the ingredients are well mixed but don't overdo it - it won't hurt if it's a bit lumpy. Let it sit for 10 minutes or so and then oil a frying pan or griddle and when it's hot, add small spoons of the batter to make the pancakes. When bubbles form on the top and the edges look drier, flip it and cook on the other side. Serve with fruit and a little icing sugar.

Stage One serve as small strips, with fruit purée
Stage Two offer slightly larger pieces and choped fruit
Stage Three your baby can hold a whole one and eat it

Baby-Led Tip

A great way to serve these is to wrap one around a banana, then cut it into pieces. It's like a fruity, pancake sushi roll!

Homemade Apple Sauce

A jar of apple sauce can be used for lots of different things. It adds sweetness to cake and biscuit recipes in place of sugar, it can be added to yoghurt or vegan ice cream as a pudding and of course it is ideal as a first food when starting your weaning repertoire.

Ingredients

2 fresh, sweet apples, washed, peeled and cored
Juice of half a lemon
About 4 tbsp water

What to do

Place the apple, cut into chunks or diced, into a small saucepan and add the water and lemon juice. Gently cook on the stove top until the apple is soft and tender. Next, place into a mini food blender or mash well with a fork until you have a smooth texture. Keeps in the fridge for a couple of days.

Scrambled Tofu

A lovely alternative to scrambled eggs, this uses tofu for protein and adds a colourful batch of vegetables for additional vitamins.

Ingredients

1 small onion, chopped
4 tbsp red, yellow and orange peppers plus courgettes, all diced
280g firm tofu
1 tbsp nutritional yeast
2 tbsp olive oil
½ tsp garlic powder
½ tsp turmeric

What to do

Sauté the onion; when it starts to soften, add the peppers and courgettes. In a blender, put a quarter of the tofu, the milk, nutritional yeast and spices and blend. The turmeric turns it a nice yellow. Crumble the rest of the tofu into the vegetables, cook for a few minutes then add the liquid and cook for a further five minutes.

Sweetcorn Fritters

These are tasty and filling and can be picked up with little hands. They are good for breakfast, lunch, dinner or a snack.

Ingredients

2 cups plain flour
1 tin sweetcorn or 340g frozen corn
1 tsp vegan stock powder
2 tbsp vegan nutritional yeast with added B12
½ bunch of chives
150 ml organic soya milk or oat milk (unsweetened)
80g firm or silken tofu

What to do

Blend the tofu and milk to a smooth liquid. Cut the chives into very short lengths. Mix the dry ingredients together, then add the corn and chives. Add the liquid to the dry ingredients and mix well. You may need to add some extra milk to get to the right consistency; thick but falling easily from a spoon. Heat a large frying pan and add a little olive oil. When it's hot, add small spoonfulls to the pan and cook on a low heat until the inside is cooked through and the outside is crispy.

Suitable for

Stage Three and Baby-Led Weaning

Idea: serve with a dip, such as coconut yoghurt or a low sugar tomato ketchup.

Mini Strawberry Pancakes

Eveyone loves pancakes for breakfast and thse little treats will appeal to your little one with their fruity taste and baby-sized portions.

Ingredients

150g plain flour
2 tsp baking powder
1 tbsp caster sugar
1 tsp vanilla extract
200ml oat milk
Half a punnet of ripe strawberries, blended to a purée, plus a few extra for eating, halved and with the stalks removed
A little icing sugar to serve

What to do

Mix together all the ingredients and stir until well blended. Leave to sit for 10 minutes or so and then heat a frying pan. Drizzle in a little olive or rapeseed oil and when heated, pour in little teaspoons of the batter. Cook until bubbles appear on the surface, then flip and cook on the other side. Cook these in batches until all the batter is used, then serve hot or cool with some strawberry pieces.

Stage One slice the pancakes into small strips
Stage Two offer halves of pancake and halved strawberries
Stage Three your baby can eat a whole pancake

Serving Tip

If you have the time, it's fun to make three colours of these sweet treats. Divide the batter into 3 bowls, mix 2 teaspoons of strawberry purée into one bowl, 5 into the second and leave the last plain.

Avocado Smash With Toppings

All vegans eat avocado on toast, right? Well, it may be a cliché but it's delicious and has many great nutrients too. Try these different ways to enjoy these delightful green fruits, while introducing your little one to new tastes and textures. You can use the different toppings to introduce different vitamins, minerals or protein.

Ingredients

The base:
½ an avocado
Piece of wholemeal bread
2 tsp olive oil
Lime juice
Pinch of black pepper
1/4 tsp salt

The toppings:
Mixed seeds, finely ground
Ripe red and yellow cherry tomatoes, chopped
Cress, pea shoots or micro greens
Flax seeds
Fresh apricot slices
Pine nuts
Cucumber slices
Black sesame seeds
Vegan feta-style cheese
Toasted sweetcorn

What to do

Classic:
Toast the bread and cut it into little sticks, just the right size for baby hands. Mash the avocado with the oil, lime juice, salt and pepper. Spread the mix on top of the toast sticks. Serve at once, as avocado goes brown if left for too long.

Topped:
Add one or more of the toppings on each piece of toast so that your little one can choose the ones they find most appealing.

Toast swaps:
Try sourdough, rye bread or any other kind of bread that you can slice and then cut into little

Sushi Avo: For a twist, flatten some leftover cold sushi rice in a baking tin and then cut it into little squares. Place a teaspoon of the avocado on the rice and the extra toppings of your choice.

Apricot Yoghurt Pot

There are days when you are more than happy to spend hours creating delicious new recipes for your baby. Other days, all you want is a quick, easy and of course nutritious option for your little one. This yoghurt pot is ideal and you can use any soft fruit, quickly puréed and served with a dairy-free yoghurt. Vegetarians can use cow's or goat's milk yoghurt.

Ingredients

4 ripe apricots, stoned
4-6 tbsp coconut yoghurt or soya yoghurt

Try this with other fruits when they are in season

What to do

After washing and stoning the apricots, place them in your baby food blender and blitz until they make a smooth purée. Layer the fruit and yoghurt, or mix together. Obviously, don't offer your baby a glass jar to serve it in - this is just to show you how lovely it looks!

Saksuka

Many types of Saksuka, or Shakshuka, exist and everyone has their own favourite way of cooking this delicious dish. I prefer to use ripe red peppers and sweet tomatoes and I cook them for so long that they become soft, gooey and unctuous. Serve with soft bread. Vegetarians can top this dish with eggs broken into the pan with the Saksuka, then cooked until set. This meal will make enough for two adults and one hungry baby.

Ingredients

4 red peppers
2 large red onions
3 tbsp olive oil
1 tsp ground cumin
1 tsp black pepper
1 clove garlic
½ tsp smoked paprika
1 tbsp tomato purée
½ bunch fresh coriander

Optional:
Free range, organic eggs
Yoghurt (dairy or vegan)

What to do

In a large frying pan, warm the olive oil and then add the sliced onions. Cook on a low heat until they become transparent - you don't want to brown them. Then add the finely sliced peppers and all the other ingredients except the coriander. Continue to cook slowly for around 30-40 minutes, stirring occasionally. When they are completely soft and the vegetables are blending together, add the coriander and you can if you wish break the eggs onto the surface, then cook for a further eight minutes. If liked, swirl over some yoghurt too.

Stage One remove your baby's portion and blend it until smooth
Stage Two chop baby's portion finely
Stage Three you can offer this more roughly chopped

Smoothies and Smoothie Bowls

You'll have seen many different colours and varieties of smoothie around and they are great ways to add fruit (and fibre) to your baby's diet. Add your favourite plant milk and fruit, then pack a punch with an added protein, fruit or flavour ingredient.; try a different one each time. It's difficult to blend just a tiny amount for your little one, so make one for baby and one each for you and your partner too. Make it fully blended for first weaning tastes and leave larger pieces of fruit as your baby gets used to textures.

Ingredients

Smoothie bowl base:
¼ cup plant milk
2 tbsp oats
½ banana
For a smoothie:
add 500 ml oat milk

What to do

Blend the milk, oats and banana in a food processor or blender. If you want to have a drinkable smoothie, add the extra plant milk. If not, it's a spoonable consistency. Then add your toppings!

All Star Toppings

Chia seeds
Nut butter
Vanilla essence
Ground almonds
Milled seed mix, hemp seeds
Cinnamon, nutmeg, cardamom
Kale
Granola
Apple sauce
Mango
Figs and dates
Puffed rice or cornflakes
Sunflower seeds

Nuts & grated coconut
Frozen raspberries, strawberries, blackberries, blueberries or blackcurrants
Peaches and apricots
Pineapple chunks
Kiwi fruit
Avocado
Cocoa powder
Orange juice
Baby spinach
Milled organic seeds
Coconut or soya yoghurt

Blue Banana

Add blueberries to the milk, oats and banana. Top with blueberries, banana slices and strawberries plus some organic milled seeds with goji berries.

Mango Madness

Put some fresh mango and frozen apricots in the mix. Top with sliced kiwi fruit, strawberries and oats.

Pink Protein

Add a small handful of raspberries and a teaspoon of almond butter. Top with chia seeds and raspberries.

Lunch or Dinner

Fresh Borlotti Bean and Carrot Purée

The carrots in this tasty purée offer great vitamins including A which is good for the eyes and the beans offer protein, making this a filling and nutritious meal.

Ingredients

2 carrots
Handful of fresh Borlotti beans, freshly podded
Sprig of curly parsley

What to do

Cut the carrot into batons, about 5 cm long. Steam them until tender (8-10 minutes) and then for the last 3-4 minutes of cooking, add the beans. When they vegetables are cooked and soft, remove them from the steamer and reserve some batons and beans for baby-led weaning. Blend the rest with a little water and the parsley.

Stage One make a very smooth purée
Stage Two allow the mixture to still have a little texture
Stage Three you can roughly mash the veg with a fork

Baby-led Tip

You could serve this on its own for one of your baby's first meals, or you could add extra elements to make a complete meal. Offer some toast or pitta bread sticks for your baby to dip into it, or let him use the carrot batons to scoop up the purée.

Offer some cooked
vegetables for a baby-led
weaning approach

Green Bean Purée

This can be used in the Risotto Recipe on page 108. You can use green beans, Bobby beans, Kenya beans – any fresh, in-season bean variety will do.

Ingredients

Handful of green beans with tops and stalks removed, washed and chopped.
Remove any woody side

What to do

Place the beans in a baby food processor and steam until tender, then blend with a little of the cooking water and a small knob of vegan butter.

Baby-led Tip

When you have steamed the beans, reserve a few and offer them to your baby so that she can feed herself. This purée can also be used in a risotto, pasta or served as a side dish at other meals.

Aubergine Purée

This is a good low-maintenance, stand-by dish that can be fed to your baby on its own, or used in a pasta sauce or as a baby version of Moussaka or Iman Bayildi.

Ingredients

1 aubergine
1 tbsp olive oil
½ garlic clove (optional)
2 tbsp vegan yoghurt

What to do

Place a whole, washed aubergine on a baking tray, having pricked it all over with a fork. Roast for 40 minutes at 200⁰. Remove from the oven and when cooled, peel off the skin and mash the flesh with the oil and garlic for a tasty dip. You can add the yoghurt if you like too.

Tip

Make sure that the aubergine is really, really soft - this is one vegetable that is not very nice raw.

Fennel and Apple Purée with Dill

Don't be afraid to mix fruit and vegetables when trying out new tastes with your baby. The sweetness of a fruit can often help them to accept a new vegetable flavour and the flavours together can be more than a sum of their parts!

Ingredients

½ a young, tender fennel bulb
One sweet apple
Tiny sprig of dill

What to do

Place the fennel and apple in a baby food processor and steam until tender, then blend with a little of the cooking water and the dill.

Stage One: blend to a smooth purée
Stage Two: Leave this meal slightly chunky
Stage Three: chop roughly

Baby-led Tip

Retain some of the fennel and apple pieces after cooking and let your baby taste and munch them.

Parsnip and Cream Cheese Dip

When parsnips are in season, they are sweet and nutty and just plain delicious. They can be used in lots of ways and are inexpensive too.

Ingredients

2 parsnips
2 tbsp vegan cream cheese – we like Violife's Creamy Original Flavour.
A drizzle of olive oil such as Zaytoun Fairtrade oil

What to do

Clean, peel and top and tail the parsnips and cut into chunky chip sized pieces. Steam until just tender and keep a few back. Blend the rest with the cream cheese, adding a little of the cooking water if needed or a little plant milk. Drizzle the top with the olive oil and allow your little one to dip in with some of the parsnip sticks, or some bread or toast sticks. Pitta works well too.

Suitable for: Stage Three and Baby-Led Weaning

Avocado Pesto Spiral Pasta

Pasta is a favourite for adults and kids alike and there are so many shapes that you can really have fun. Start with tiny pasta shapes and progress to chunkier versions like fusilli.

Ingredients

Bunch of basil leaves
Half an avocado
Piece of vegan parmesan-style cheese, finely grated
Two shallots, finely chopped
Handful of pine nuts
½ a carton vegan cream cheese
Use tiny star pasta (stelline), then farfalline or orzo, progressing to fusilli and penne pasta (check it's egg-free)

What to do

Sauté the shallots in olive oil and meanwhile boil the pasta according to the packet instructions. Put the basil, avocado, cheese and cream cheese into a small blender and pulse until mixed thoroughly and the herbs are chopped well. Remove from the blender and stir a spoon or two through the hot, drained pasta – there's just enough heat to allow the sauce to warm through. Add the pine nuts (toasted if possible to release the flavour) over the top just before serving and another sprinkle of the parmesan style cheese.

Stage One blend the sauce including the pine nuts to a smooth purée and serve with fine pasta
Stage Two leave the sauce slightly chunky and offer with small sized pasta shapes
Stage Three offer with larger pasta shapes like penne and fusilli

Baby-led Tip

Allow your baby to feed himself pieces of the pasta.

Macaroni Cheese

Whether you call it this or the more American Mac N Cheese, it's always a favourite – especially when you veganise it! The nutritional yeast makes it magically taste of cheese. This sauce can also be used over cauliflower or as a sauce on its own.

Ingredients

1 onion, finely chopped
Half tbsp vegan bouillon stock powder
1 tbsp plain flour
2 tbsp nutritional yeast
½ a carton of oat milk
Handful of breadcrumbs
Small sized macaroni

Give it a twist

To add protein to this favourite, add edamame or cannelini beans

Cashew Version

Another sauce version using
cashews.
1 ½ cups raw cashews, soaked in water overnight
Juice of ½ lemon
3 tbsp nutritional yeast
1 cup oat milk
½ tsp each of turmeric & mustard
Blend until it makes a good sauce.

What to do

Cook the macaroni. Meanwhile, fry the onion in some oil and then add the flour, yeast and stock powder and cook it for a few minutes to cook out the flour and create a roux. Slowly add the milk, a little at a time to avoid lumps. When done, pour the sauce over the pasta and mix, then sprinkle the top with the breadcrumbs. Cook in the over at 200^{0} for 15-20 minutes until golden and bubbling.

Suitable for:

Stage Three and Baby-Led Weaning; you could mash or blend for Stages One and Two.

Baby-led Tip

Your baby will love to pick up pieces of the pasta and feed herself. Use the smaller types of pasta recommended on page 91 for younger babies.

Easy Hummus

A good hummus is a great stand-by. Whether you soak the chickpeas yourself or buy them in tins, this is a nutritious snack and very popular with little ones.

Ingredients

200g cooked chickpeas
Olive oil
2 tbsp tahini

What to do

Blend the ingredients together in a baby food blender. Serve on its own, or with bread sticks, pitta or toast fingers or vegetable sticks.

Spinach And Potato Purée

This is a very simple dish that can be used as a first weaning meal or can be used as a side dish with the Baby Burgers on page 113.

Ingredients

Bunch of organic spinach
2 medium potatoes; Charlottes or Reds are good

Baby-led Tip

Retain some of the potato pieces and spinach leaves and offer to your baby.

What to do

Peel the potatoes, cut them into chunks. Place in a saucepan, cover with water and boil until tender. Just as they are ready, place a sieve or colander on top of the pan with the spinach in it. Cook for a couple more minutes with a lid on to wilt the spinach. Drain, then blend with a little of the cooking water. This makes a good batch so you can freeze some for later meals.

Stage One blend to a smooth purée
Stage Two leave this meal slightly chunky
Stage Three chop roughly

All The Greens

One of the best ways to get vitamins into your baby is to offer a good mix of vegetables and fruit and this brightly coloured purée used three nutritious ingredients.

Ingredients

Handful of kale leaves
Stem of broccoli
½ a small, tender fennel bulb

What to do

Wash and chop all three of the veg and place in a steamer. Cook until the broccoli stems and fennel are tender. Then add a knob of vegan butter and blend with a little of the cooking water – this may take some time as broccoli is quite grainy.

Stage One blend to a smooth purée
Stage Two leave this meal slightly chunky
Stage Three chop roughly

Baby-led Tip

Retain some fist-sized pieces to offer to your baby.

Roasted Red Pepper And Tomato Purée

This is one dish that you can use to make lunch for the whole family; when you have cooked the vegetables, remove a small amount for your baby's meal, then turn the rest into a nourishing soup by adding some vegan stock.

Ingredients

4 red peppers
8 very ripe large tomatoes
Red onion
4 cloves of garlic, in their skins

What to do

Wash and chop the onion, peppers and tomatoes, then place in a roasting tin with a drizzle of olive oil and the cloves of garlic, still in their little jackets. Roast at 200^0 until the veg are soft and tender – about 30 to 40 minutes. Remove the skins from the garlic and add back to the vegetables.

Stage One take a tomato and half a pepper and blend in a mini food processor with a little of one of the cloves of garlic, squeezed from its skin.

Stage Two & Three there are two great options here. Either use the purée as a dip with some toast or pitta fingers, or simply slice the peppers and tomatoes finely, rub some toast fingers with a piece of the garlic, then top with the vegetables.

For the family squeeze out all the garlic, add that with the roasted vegetables to a pan and add enough vegan stock to cover. When brought to the boil, simmer for a few minutes and then blend to make a delicious soup. Serve with a swirl of coconut yoghurt and some fresh, chopped coriander.

Sunshine Squash

This dish offers the best of both the nutritious, vitamin-packed vegetables plus the protein from the lentils.

Ingredients

1 large organic carrot
¼ butternut squash
½ cup red lentils, cooked
¼ tsp cumin
A few sprigs of parsley
½ tsp vegan low sodium stock powder

What to do

Cut the carrot and squash into chunks and steam until tender. Place the vegetables with the lentils and parsley in a blender and add the stock powder, cumin and 4-6 tbsp water. Blend until smooth. Add a small chunk of vegan butter and stir well.

Baby-led Tip: Retain some of the vegetables and offer to baby.

Butternut Squash And Lentil Puree

This has a Stage One, Two and Three option with baby-led ideas

Ingredients

½ butternut squash
200g cooked green lentils
¼ chopped red onion

Stage One: blend to a smooth purée
Stage Two: leave chunky
Stage Three: chop roughly

Baby-led Tip

Retain some of the squash and offer to your baby.

What to do

Peel the squash and remove the seeds. Then cut it into chunky sticks, the size of chunky cut chips. Steam the squash until soft and keep some of the chunks for your baby to feed themselves. Cook the onion in a little olive oil, then add the lentils and squash. When they have all heated through, blend the mixture with a little of the cooking water and the coriander. For Stage Two, leave the mixture with some little lumps or keep blending for a smooth, Stage One purée.

Creamy Squash and Carrot

A nice alternative purée with a luxurious touch of plant based cream. You could also use a vegan cream cheese.

Ingredients

One carrot
½ small yellow squash
4 tbsp soya cream

What to do

Peel and chop the squash and carrot, then steam until soft. Blend with the soya cream.

Stage One: blend to a smooth purée
Stage Two: leave chunky
Stage Three: chop roughly

Baby-led Tip: Retain some of the vegetables and offer to baby.

Green Goodness

A clutch of gorgeous green vegetables with the zing of mint.

Ingredients

A handful of cabbage leaves
A handful of freshly podded peas
A floret of broccoli
An apple
A sprig of mint leaves
A sprig of fresh coriander

Stage One: blend to a smooth purée
Stage Two: leave chunky
Stage Three: chop roughly

What to do

This is the kind of meal you can make your baby when you have a few pieces of vegetables left over from last night's dinner. In this case, we used three vegetables plus a crunchy apple to give a touch of sweetness and some extra vitamins. Steam the vegetables, starting with the broccoli and then adding the cabbage and finally the peas and apple. When all is tender, blend with a little of the cooking water and the herbs.

Best Ever Baby Tomato Sauce

This sweet and delicious tomato sauce can be used in a wide variety of ways; as a pasta sauce, in a bean chilli, for the stuffed cabbage recipe on page 113, as a dip, as a base for a smooth tomato soup and more. It has a hit of protein from the lentils, plus the vitamins and sweetness from the tomatoes. Experiment with adding different herbs like basil and parsley and perhaps a hint of a spice like cumin.

Ingredients

Ten very ripe cherry vine tomatoes
One banana shallot
½ cup of red lentils, cooked
Sprig of coriander leaves
2 tbsp olive oil
Pinch of black pepper

What to do

Chop the onions very finely and then sauté them in the olive oil until they are very soft, then add the tomatoes, quartered, and put the lid on. Place them on a very low gas and keep cooking and stirring until they are broken down and soft. Next, add the cooked lentils, pepper and coriander. Blend the sauce until smooth and use over pasta.

Alternative Option:

Buttermato Sauce

Make the sauce as above but while it's still cooking, steam or roast a few chunks of peeled and de-seeded butternut squash. When it is soft, mash or blend it until smooth. Add this squash purée to the tomato sauce for a secret added vegetable but more importantly, a delicious taste and texture.

Butternut Squash, Cauliflower and Cannellini Bean Mash

A filling and vibrant mix of vegetables and beans.

Ingredients

¼ butternut squash, pelled and de-seeded
A handful of cauliflower florets
½ can of low sodium cannellini beans or around 200 g pre-cooked beans

What to do

Peel and cut the squash into chunky sticks and cut the florets of cauliflower into baby-sized pieces. Place them in a steamer and cook until tender. Reserve some of the pieces for baby-led weaning. Place the cooked squash and cauliflower into a blender with the beans and a little of the cooking water and blend to the consistency for your stage.

Baby-led Tip

Retain some pieces to offer to your baby.

Roasted Red Pepper, Cashew And Cauliflower Mix

A filling and vibrant mix of vegetables and beans.

Ingredients

A packet of raw cashew nuts
Two to three red peppers
A few florets of cauliflower

Baby-led Tip

Retain some pieces to offer to your baby.

What to do

Soak the cashew in water for at least four hours, or overnight. Roast the peppers in the oven until the skins looks wrinkled. Take them out of the oven and when it's cool enough, you will be able to peel the skin off. Steam the cauliflower until tender. Leave some pieces of vegetables cut to baby hand size chunks for baby-led weaning.

Stage One: blend to a smooth purée
Stage Two: leave it chunky
Stage Three: chop roughly

Baby Caponata

A fairly grown-up taste but one your baby will probably enjoy and it's a great dish for the whole family. Though I wouldn't usually recommend adding sugary things to baby food, this gives the caponata its distinctive sweet-sour flavour and I have kept the amount of sweetener to a minimum.

Ingredients

1 aubergine, chopped into very fine cubes
1 onion, chopped finely
A good squeeze of tomato purée
4 ripe vine tomatoes, chopped
1 tbsp apple cider vinegar
1 tsp maple syrup
Optional extras; green or black olives, capers, raisins, pine nuts

What to do

Sauté the onion in olive oil until soft and then add the aubergine. Keep cooking slowly until the aubergine is soft – this may take some time and you'll need patience - if it looks as if it is sticking, add a small splash of water. Once it is deliciously soft and gooey, add the tomato purée and the tomatoes, plus the vinegar and syrup; keep stirring. When it is all cooked through, you can serve it as it is or pile it on top of toast pieces or pitta bread sticks. Add the olives, chopped, and raisins and capers if liked.

Stage One: blend baby's portion finely
Stage Two and Three: make sure the vegetables are chopped finely

Baby-led Tip

Allow your little one to pick up the mixture or offer a spoon.

Lentil Stew

Warming and hearty, this is a great way to add protein to your child's diet in an easy to cook and eat way. The vegetables add vitamins. Add some you know your baby loves and slip in a new

Ingredients

Cup of puy lentils
½ onion
One carrot
One stick of celery
Tomato purée, two tbsp
½ tsp cumin
½ tsp dry oregano

Suitable for: Stage One, blend. Stage Two and Three, chop finely.

What to do

Sauté the onion, the add the other vegetables. When soft, add the herbs and spices and then the lentils. Add a couple of tbsp of the purée – you want this mixture to be quite dry, not too wet. Keep cooking and stirring until it's rich and gooey. Finally, garnish with the parsley, finely chopped.

Tip

Use in the Stuffed Cabbage on page 113 or as a yummy base for a mini Shepherd's Pie.

Broad Beans & Cream Cheese On Toast

A great and delicious lunch that has a good mix of vitamins, some fibre, protein and carbs for energy. Make for the whole family.

Ingredients

Large bag of broad beans, podded, or a bag of frozen beans
Tub of soya cream cheese
Wholemeal or sourdough bread, toasted and sliced

What to do

Take the beans and steam for a few minutes. If you can be bothered, slip the skins off the beans. This gives a smoother purée. Mash the beans well, then stir in a teaspoon or two of the cream cheese until well mixed. Toast a slice of bread, then cut off the crusts and cut it into sticks.

Options: Leave beans whole for a toddler or serve them mashed or puréed for younger babies.

Swedish Style Balls

Great toddler snacks, these little balls of protein are great hot or cold, with mashed potatoes, with our tomato sauce or in a lunch box. You can even use leftover ones squished into a bun to make an instant burger with tomato relish. This recipe makes a big batch, so you can use some today and some tomorrow.

Ingredients

1 tin lentils or 400g cooked lentils
2 tbsp plain flour
½ tsp mixed dried herbs
½ tsp cumin
Small bowl breadcrumbs
Olive oil for frying

Tip

Try panko breadcrumbs for extra crunch

What to do

Put the lentils into a large bowl and using a potato masher or fork, mash about three quarters of them, leaving the rest whole. Add the other dry ingredients and mix well. With wet hands, form the mixture into little balls and then roll them in the breadcrumbs. Fry in shallow oil until the outside is crisp and the inside cooked; alternatively, roll in a little oil and cook in the oven.

Suitable for

Stage Three and Baby-Led Weaning

Green Risotto

Use the Green Bean Purée from page 86 for this.

Ingredients

Finely chopped shallot
½ cup risotto rice
Cup of vegan stock
Green bean purée plus some cooked whole beans

What to do

Cook the shallot in olive oil, then add the rice and stir until each grain is coated with the hot oil. Gradually add the stock, a little at a time until it has all been absorbed and the rice is cooked. Finally, add the Green Bean Purée and mix.

Stage One: blend to a smooth purée
Stage Two: leave the rice as it is and chop the beans
Stage Three: serve with whole or half beans

Baby-led Tip

Offer your baby some of the whole or halved beans to pick up and eat and give her a spoon to start trying to feed herself.

Rainbow Risotto

Once your little one has got used to risotto, you can use different vegetables each time. Start with favourites, then add some new tastes. You could also add some pulses and top with vegan cheese.

Ingredients

½ onion
½ each of a red and yellow pepper
Handful of green beans
One carrot
Handful of frozen peas
Cup of risotto rice

What to do

Sauté the onion in a little olive oil, then add the peppers, carrots and beans, chopped into small similar sized pieces, for 10 minutes. Meanwhile, cook the risotto rice in the stock according to the packet instructions. When the vegetables are soft, add the peas and then stir them into the rice.

Stage One: blend to a smooth purée
Stage Two: leave the rice as it is and chop the vegetables finely
Stage Three: offer some chunks of veg for baby to feed himself

Baby Burgers

These fun sized baby burgers are a good way to introduce some hidden vegetables and they are high in protein too thanks to both nuts and lentils. Sreve them with some home made potato wedges or in a bun with tomato ketchup.

Ingredients

1 red onion, finely chopped
1 stick each of celery and carrot, finely chopped
4-5 green beans, steamed then finely chopped
1 cup dry weight of cooked lentils (any colour)
½ cup raw cashews
½ tsp cumin
½ tsp ground coriander
1 tbsp ground linseed, mixed with 3 tbsp warm water to make vegan 'egg'
breadcrumbs

What to do

Sauté the onion until soft and then add the carrot and celery, plus the spices and keep cooking to blend the flavours and cook the vegetables. Add the cashews and lentils and stir well. Put into a blender and blitz until you have a smooth consistency. Place the linseed 'egg' in one bowl and the breadcrumbs in another. Form the mix into little balls and flatten slightly, then dip first into the linseed mixture and then the bread-crumbs. Fry in a little olive oil on both sides until cooked through and the outsides are crispy.

Serve in mini burger buns with some slices of tomato and some crunchy green lettuce and low-sugar ketchup.

Suitable for

Stage Three and Baby-Led Weaning

Store Cupboard Healthy Baked Beans

It's late, there's not much in the house for lunch or dinner and you're tired. Instead of reaching for a tin of ready-made baked beans, which are often full of salt and sugar, this is a really quick and easy way to make beans that are tasty and healthy.

Ingredients

1 tin organic mixed beans
1 tin cannellini beans
1 tin organic chopped tomatoes
1 tbsp organic tomato purée
A few splashes of vegan Worcestershire sauce

What to do

Fry the onion in a little olive oil and when it's golden and a bit transparent, throw in all the rest of the ingredients. The longer you cook this, the tastier it is as the tomatoes get rich and gooey. Serve the classic way with toast or over rice, couscous or quinoa.

Stage One: blend to a smooth purée
Stage Two: chop the beans up roughly with a fork
Stage Three: offer as it is, allo baby to feed himself

Stuffed Cabbage Leaves

Using the lentil stew recipe from page 106, this is a rich and satisfying meal for babies and for all the family.

Ingredients

The outer leaves from a Savoy cabbage; lentil stew, jar of organic tomato sauce or our recipe on page 100; Grated vegan mozzarella style cheese.

What to do

Boil a pan of water and add the cabbage leaves, a few at a time. Cook for 5-6 minutes to soften. Cool enough to handle and cut out sturdy stems. Place a spoonful of the lentil mix into a leaf, then roll up, tucking in the sides to form a neat parcel. Repeat with all leaves. Place in an oven-proof dish and top with the tomato sauce. Bake at 200^0 for 20 minutes, covered with foil, until hot through. Remove the foil and sprinkle cheese over the top and return to the over for a further 7-10 minutes until the cheese is melted and bubbling.

n In The Oven Pizza

This is another great use for our tomato sauce and it uses bits and pieces of vegetable that may be left in the bottom of the fridge. It's also a great way to get your child interested in cooking, as they can help you make the little pizzas, choosing their own toppings. Place them all in little bowls and let your child choose - they may well

Ingredients

Soft bread rolls, halved
Tomato sauce
Vegan mozzarella

Suggested toppings:

Sweetcorn
Peas
Red onions
Chopped tomatoes
Olives, green or black
Celery, chopped up small
parsley and coriander

What to do

Place the rolls with the cut sides up on a baking tray. Spread the top with a spoonful of our tomato sauce (see page 100) and then arrange the other toppings in some small bowls. Get your little one to help you add the toppings - don't be too precious about it, as it's likely to be a little bit messy! Sprinkle the tops with some vegan cheese and pop into a hot oven (about 180^{0}) for 10-15 minutes until the cheese has melted and the vegetables are cooked.

Vegetarian option: add some grated dairy mozzarella or cheddar

Suitable for

Stage Three and
Baby-Led Weaning

What To Do With Tofu

Tofu is, of course, a great ingredient for your vegan child's diet and there are lots of ways to cook it and include it as an ingredient. What's so great about it? Well, it contains a lot of protein and all of the nine essential amino acids. Iron and calcium are in the mix too plus vitamin B1 and minerals phosphorous, magnesium, copper, zinc and manganese. For most of the recipes, use a block of what is called firm tofu (not silken, though the latter is great for sauces, smoothies and more) and it's best to press it before you use it. Simply wrap in a clean, dry tea towel, place on a board and leave a heavy iron pan or some books on top of it for at least 20 minutes. The other thing to remember is that it does not have much of a taste, so add your own!

Use as an ingredient

You can add any kind of tofu to a pasta sauce for extra protein. Place some tofu in a small blender with a splash of oat or soya milk and blend to a thick consistency. Alternatively, crumble or grate firm tofu straight into a sauce for a Bolognese-like dish. You can also add tofu to a lovely fruity smoothie. Experiment with different recipes!

Baked Tofu Fingers

You can cut firm tofu into baby-sized slices after pressing, then add some tasty flavours to tempt your little one. Brush the slices with a teaspoon of brown barley Miso, mixed with a little warm water - or just use your finger to smear it on! Bake the fingers in the oven on a greased tray for 10 minutes each side and serve cool or warm. You can also try teryaki, soy sauce or hoisin; use sparingly, as they can be quite high in salt.

Tofu Tots

These little golden bites will be a big hit with your tot. Slice the tofu into nugget-sized chunks. Put in a bowl with a splash of soya milk and stir to coat. Mix cornflour or plain flour with ¼ tsp garlic or onion powder, ¼ tsp turmeric and a little paprika. Add this to the tofu, stir again to coat each piece and then bake or shallow fry for 10 minutes per side. Serve with a healthy tomato sauce or another dip. As an alternatively to the flour mix, you can use breadcrumbs instead for added crunch.

Tofubabs

Dice some tofu, then slide the chunks onto skewers (soak these first to avoid having them burn) with a mix of chopped onions, peppers, tomatoes, courgettes and whatever vegetables you fancy. Grill the kebabs or cook them on a barbecue, brushed with a marinade of your choice. Sesame oil and a low sodium soy sauce works well. Make sure you remove the skewers before giving the tofu and vegetables to your little one.

Tofu Japanese Patties

Using the fine side of a grater, grate a block of firm tofu, an onion and a carrot, plus a clove of garlic and some ginger. Next, add some finely chopped chives and season lightly. Add 1 tbsp plain flour and then mix all the ingredients well together. With wet hands, form into little cakes and press down on both sides so that they will cook evenly. Shallow fry the cakes on both sides until golden and serve with a dip.

Cashew And Carrot Loaf

Ingredients

400g raw cashews
2 carrots
1 onion
2 small garlic cloves
1 tsp mixed dried herbs
½ tbsp stock powder
2 slices bread (this is great for using up stale bread)
Tbsp mixed seeds
59 ml olive oil

Suitable for

Stage Three and Baby-Led Weaning

What to do

This is best made in a food processor (though you can finely chop everything by hand). Put the carrots, onions and garlic in with a chopping blade in place and blitz until they are very finely chopped. Add the bread, nuts, stock powder and herbs and keep the machine going until everything resembles fine bread-crumbs. Put into a greased loaf tin and roast for about 40 minutes on 180⁰. Serve with mashed potato and other veg purées on the side, just like a proper roast dinner. This makes enough for a family of four.

Mini Rhubarb Tarts

Make for the whole family when this is in season. The apple helps sweeten the rather sharp taste of rhubarb without the need for extra sugar.

Ingredients

5-8 sticks rhubarb
2 sweet apples like Braeburn
Shop bought short crust pastry (check it's vegan)
Carton of soya custard

What to do

Wash and chop the rhubarb, peel and core the apples and cut into small pieces. Cook them together in a little water – you really don't need much as long as you use a heavy pan and keep the lid tight on. When they are just soft (don't over do it), take off the heat. Cut out some circles of pastry and push into the depressions in a bun tin. Prick them all over and bake blind for 8 minutes. Allow to cool, spoon a little of the custard into each tart and top with the fruit.

Suitable for

Stage Three and Baby-Led Weaning

Apple and Blackberry Puddings

Ingredients

One large Bramley apple or a similar variety
A bowl of freshly picked blackberries - make sure to check them all over individually for stalks, dirt and insects and wash well.
Juice of half a lemon
2 tbsp sugar

What to do

Peel and core the apple, cut into chunks. Place the chunks in a steamer or pan and with a little water, the juice and sugar. Steam until just soft – you don't want to overdo it so they are falling apart. Reserve some of the chunks for Baby-Led Weaning. Add the blackberries to the apple and purée.

Suitable for

Stage One: offer your baby the fibely blended purée
Stage Two: Mash the fruit, leaving some texture and small lumpsStage Three: Just serve as it comes from the pot.

Baby-led Tip

Your little one can pick up and taste the apple pieces and the berries - you may want to cut larger ones in half.

Serving tips and additional recipes

There are lots of ways to use a fruit purée or compote like this:

- Serve alone
- Serve with an oat or rice-based porridge, or with a soya yoghurt from eight months or dairy yoghurt from 12 months.
- Alternatively, use this as a base for a delicious fruit crumble, served with some vegan custard or ice cream; see our crumble topping recipe on page 133.

Mango Madness

One of the simplest deserts is a fruit purée on top of some coconut or soya yoghurt.

Ingredients

1 ripe mango or a tin of mango purée (Alfonso mangoes are amazingly sweet if you can catch them in season)
A carton of coconut or soya yoghurt

What to do

Peel and stone a mango, then blend until it's a smooth and delicious purée. Put a couple of teaspoons of coconut or soya yoghurt into a bowl and top with the mango.

Suitable for

Stage One, Two and Three and Baby-Led Weaning

Quick and Easy Focaccia Bread

This delicious bread was inspired the late great Antonio Carluccio and is great to have with a dip, hummus, soup or as the base for a pizza. This quantity makes two large pizza bases; make some for today and freeze the rest.

Ingredients

50g bread flour
1 sachet or 7g dried yeast
1 tsp sugar
1 tsp salt
300 ml warm water
4 tbsp olive oil

What to do

Put the flour and salt in a food processor with a dough hook or soft plastic blade. Pule to disperse the salt. In a jug, mix the yeast, warm water and oil and leave until it foams on top. Mix the liquid into the flour with the processor on low and let it knead for 7 minutes. Leave, covered, in a bowl for 1 hour, then tip onto a baking ray and leave for another 20 minutes. Bake at 200^0 for 30 minutes, then 5 minutes on 180^0.

Instant Fruit Ice Creams

A very quick, simple and refreshing dessert for those lazy summer days. Serve in a little bowl or get some nice cones. The basis for all of these varieties is frozen bananas and it's a great way to use up slightly over-ripe fruits.

Ingredients

4-6 bananas, peeled and frozen the night before, or keep some in the freezer all the time for ice cream emergencies!
4 tbsp soya milk

Varieties:

1 tsp vanilla essence
A punnet of raspberries, blueberries or strawberries
a tin of peaches, drained
Mango, peeled and stoned
1 tsp smooth nut butter
1 tsp cocoa powder
Fresh mint leaves

Or

Frozen berries, either individual or mixed fruit

What to do

For each of your chosen flavours, take one banana plus a handful of your chosen fruit or ingredient, and put them into a blender or food processor with the milk. You need quite a heavy-duty blender or processor to cope with the frozen fruit.

Suggested flavours:

Strawberry

Raspberry and coconut

Chocolate

Blueberry

Mango and peach

Mint

Suitable for

Stage One, Two and Three and Baby-Led Weaning

Upside Down Pear Muffin Cakes

Ingredients

2 pears
1 tbsp vegan butter
1 tsp brown sugar
180ml soya milk
60ml apple sauce
50ml rapeseed oil
1 tsp vanilla extract
1 tsp cinnamon
350 g self raising flour

What to do

Firstly, line the muffin tins with paper cases. Finely dice the peeled and cored pears and stir through them the sugar with a little of the cinnamon Arrange the pear to just cover the bottom of each case. Mix the wet ingredients, then the dry and stir both together – use the remainder of the cinnamon in the mix. Place a couple of spoons into each muffin tin, leaving room for them to rise. Bake for 20 minutes on 180^{0} and when a skewer comes out clean, they are done. Cool for a little while, then remove from the cases.

Blueberry Cake Bars

A tray bake is a great way to make a good batch of treats that will keep in the fridge.

Ingredients

Packet of blueberries (save a few for the topping)
150ml oat milk
2 tbsp rapeseed oil
1 tbsp apple cider vinegar
Juice of half a lemon
1 tsp baking powder
200g self raising flour

Additional topping if liked:

One small tub coconut yoghurt
Juice of the other half of the lemon
Remaining blueberries, chopped

What to do

Mix together the wet ingredients in one bowl and the dry in another, then pour the wet onto the dry and mix until fully combined. Grease a shallow baking tin and line with greaseproof paper. Pour the cake mixture in and bake at 150^0 for around 15 minutes.Remove from the tin and leave to cool. Cut into little baby-sized cake fingers. If you want to use the topping, mix together the coconut yoghurt and lemon juice and spread on top of the cake. Decorate with the reserved chopped blueberries.

Baby Banana Bread

This is great for using up over-ripe fruit and to offer some fibre in your baby's diet. There's also a little protein from the linseeds, and sweetness from the bananas. Many banana bread recipes use a lot of sugar but that's really not necessary – though if you feel it's not sweet enough, add some chopped sultanas or a little more sugar.

Ingredients

3 very ripe bananas
75g rapeseed oil
200g self raising flour
1 tsp baking powder
2 tsp cinnamon
½ tsp nutmeg
½ tbsp ground linseeds
Small handful sultanas, finely chopped
1 tbsp brown sugar

What to do

Place the ground linseeds in a bow and add 3 tbsp warm water. This creates a vegan egg substitute and helps to stick the cake together. Mix all the ingredients together, add the linseeds and mx well. Bake in a lined tin for 30-40 minutes on 180 degrees and test with a knife – when it comes out clean, it's ready. Turn it and allow to cool, then serve as little chunks your baby can feed to themselves.

Carrot, Banana and Blueberry Loaf

Another banana cake recipe that adds the fibre of the carrots and the sweetness of fresh ripe blueberries.

Ingredients

1 mashed banana
2 small carrots, finely grated
Handful of blueberries
2 cups plain flour
2 tsp baking powder
Quarter cup rapeseed oil
Quarter cup soya milk
1 tsp cinnamon
½ tsp nutmeg
½ tsp ground ginger

What to do

Mix all the dry ingredients together and then add the banana and carrot. Mix this all through and then gently fold in the blueberries so as not to damage them. bake for 20-30 minutes at 180⁰ until a skewer comes out clean when you insert it into the cake. Cool and slice into baby sized chunks.

Soft White Rolls

These cloud-like white rolls are super easy to make and it's wonderful to have the smell of fresh bread in the house. They are also used for the Bun In The Oven Pizza on page 116.

Ingredients

1 sachet or 7g dried yeast
2 tbsp sugar
1 cup warm water
1 tsp salt
4 tbsp vegan butter
450g white bread flour

What to do

Mix the yeast and sugar with the warm water and leave to sit until it looks frothy. In a food processor with a dough hook or plastic blade, put the flour and salt with the vegan butter. Pulse the processor a couple of times to mix in the butter and salt, then turn it on low and add all the liquid through the spout in one go. Run the machine for 7 minutes, then place the dough in a greased bowl and cover with clingfilm, leaving for 1 hour. Take the dough from the bowl, cover a baking tray with greaseproof paper and form the dough into 8 rolls. Place on the tray, allow to rise again for an hour, then bake for 25 minutes at 180⁰.

Vegan Scones

Perfect for afternoon tea or a picnic in the park, these little scones are attractive to little ones. Beware - they can be a little messy to eat! The only thing you need to decide is what to put on them.

Ingredients

3 cups self raising flour
½ cup vegan margarine
2 tsp baking powder
2 tsp vanilla essence
Three quarters of a cup soya or oat milk
2 tbsp caster sugar
Juice of ½ a lemon

What to do

Combine all the dry ingredients, add the liquids and mix well. Knead briefly – don't overdo this – and use a tiny cutter to make little baby sized scones. Bake at 180^0 for 18-20 minutes. Serve with some strawberries, soya yoghurt, low-sugar jams or whatever else you like!

Pumpkin Biscuits

These can be cut into fun shapes – try cats and witches for Hallowe'en and stars for Christmas!

Ingredients

225 sweet potato, peeled, steamed and mashed
159 g plain flour
½ tsp dried rosemary, finely chopped
1 dessert spoon vegan butter
50g vegan cheese

What to do

While the mashed potato is still warm, add the vegan butter and cheese to allow it to melt a bit, stir, then add the flour and rosemary. Work into a dough with your hands, then roll out on a floured board until it's about 3mm thick. Cut out some shapes and lay on a greased baking sheet. Bake at 180^0 for 15 minutes until golden. These store well and are great to take out as a snack.

Crumble Topping

Who doesn't love crumble? This one can be used over any fruit base and it has no added sugar, so it's a healthy choice. The oats mean it's not so heavy and they release energy slowly, keeping little tummies fuller for longer.

Ingredients

Juice of half an orange
Zest of half an orange
100g wholemeal flour
100g oats
80g vegan butter

What to do

Mix the ingredients together and blitz in a food processor. Alternatively, rub the butter through the flour as you would for pastry, then add the oats and mix well. Place the mix on top of any fruit purée or cooked fruit and bake for 20 minutes at 180^0.

Rice Crackers

A great recipe to use up leftover rice, this works best with sushi rice and makes a good snack for your little one.

Ingredients

Leftover cooked sushi rice

Additonal ingredients if liked, stirred through rice:
Marmite
Paprika
Pinch of turmeric

What to do

This works best when the rice has recently been cooked and is good and sticky! Take desert spoons of the rice and roll into balls using wet hands. Put these on an oiled baking tray and cover with greaseproof paper. Press another tray on top to flatten them, then bake for 20 minutes at 180^0.

Coconut Rice Pudding

Though the coconut is technically a fruit, it has been classified in some countries as a tree nut. While it's not a common cause of allergies, if you have a lot of allergies in the family, make sure you use the three day rule to check your baby is not sensitive to it. It's high in zinc, B vitamins, phosphorus, protein and iron and is high in 'good' fats too.

Ingredients

½ cup pudding rice
½ tbsp dried coconut
200ml coconut milk
200ml oat milk

Stage One: blend to a smooth purée
Stage Two and Three: Serve as it is

What to do

Soak the dried or dessicated coconut in the milk for a couple of hours to soften it. Then place the milk, coconut and rice in a saucepan and bring to the boil. Then simmer the rice until it has become very soft and absorbed the milk. Serve warm or cold.

Jelly Fruit Cups

This popular pudding is great for parties and luckily, can be vegan! It's a great way to introduce different fruits to your little one

Ingredients

Packet of vegan jelly crystals e.g. Just Whole Foods Raspberry crystals
A small handful of chopped banana, raspberry and blueberry.
You can also use other fresh or cooked fruit such as berries, or cooked harder fruits like apples.

What to do

Make the jelly according to the pack's instructions. Put some of the pieces of fruit into small plastic cups or moulds such as silicone cupcake moulds. Pour the liquid jelly in on top and then allow it to set. To serve, decorate with some more fruit and perhaps a little vegan cream or custard too.

Simple Cookies

There are lots of great vegan cookie recipes and you can experiment with different ingredients to build up a repertoire of tasty snacks that are not (always) high in sugar. Use fruit to add sweetness.

Oat and Pumpkin Cookies

Ingredients

2 cups oats
½ cup pumpkin purée
(avoid pumpkin pie filling as it is sweetened)
½ cup golden sultanas

What to do

Mix the ingredients together well, then drop spoonfulls onto a greaseproof paper-covered baking tray. Bake for 10 minutes at 200⁰.

Sandwich Cookies

Ingredients

¼ cup maple syrup
½ cup cocoa powder
¼ cup brown rice flour

Filling options:

Smooth nut butter
Slices of banana
Mashed banana and cocoa powder mixed together
Coconut yoghurt

What to do

Mix the ingredients, then take put spoonsfull and form into balls. Place on a greaseproof paper-covered baking tray and flatten. Bake for 8-10 minutes at 220⁰. When cool, sandwich them together with one of the suggested fillings to make your own version of the popular biscuit you see in the shops!

Oat and Apricot Cookies

Ingredients

1 cup oats
1 very ripe banana
2 tbsp dried apricots, finely chopped
¼ tsp cinnamon

What to do

Mash the banana and then mix in the other ingredients. Scoop a tablespoon of the mixture onto greaseproof paper on a tray and bake for 10 minutes at 180⁰.

Peanut Chocolate Cookies

Ingredients

3 very ripe bananas
½ cup smooth peanut, cashew or almond butter, unsweetened
½ cup organic Fairtrade cocoa powder

What to do

Mash the banana well, then and add the cocoa and mix slowly so as not to create clouds of powder! Next, add the nut butter and mix well - it may take a little time to get it thoroughly mixed in. Place scoops of dough onto a baking sheet. Bake at 180⁰ for 10-15 minutes.

Bakewell Cookies

Ingredients

1 cup ground almonds
1 cup white flour
2 tbsp vegan butter
½ tsp almond essence
Low sugar cherry jam

What to do

Mix the dry ingredients and add the butter - this may be easier in a food processor. Put tablespoons of the dough on a tray and make a depression in the top of each with the back of a teaspoon. bake for 12 minutes at 180⁰. When cool, add a spoonful of jam in the dip.

Easy Layered Fruit Puddings

This looks gorgeous and tastes delicious. It will become a very popular dessert with old and young alike and it's incredibly simple to make, can be prepared in advance and kept in the fridge. You can use your own home made cookies for the base, or look for a good quality vegan cookie or biscuit from your local health food store. The toppings can be made from whatever fruit you have to hand and that is ripe and in season.

Ingredients

Tub of coconut or soya yoghurt
Two biscuits or cookies per pudding - we used Biscoff
Fruit purée
Some pieces of fruit to decorate

Alternative idea

Make the ceamy part with some vegan cream cheese mixed with a teaspoon of lemon juice for a 'cheesecake.'

Suitable for:

Stage One with fruit purée, Stage Two with small pieces of fruit and Stage Three and Baby-Led weaning with larger pieces of fruit for baby to pick up.

What to do

Put the biscuits or cookies into a wide bowl and use the flat end of a rolling pin, or the back of a spoon to crush them into fine crumbs. Put them into the botton of your bowl (don't use glass for babies and kids - we have used glass here to show you the layers). Next, add the fruit purée and top with the yoghurt. Decorate the top with some pieces of fruit to make it look pretty.

Mix and Match Menu Planners

Once you have got the hang of things and your little one is eating two or three times a day, you can plan ahead to ensure that your baby is getting a good mix of al the nutrients she needs. Use these charts as a suggested starting point.

Breakfast	Lunch	Dinner
Porridge with two or three fruit purée	Carrot & courgette muffin	Sweetcorn fritters and carrot purée
Rice cereal	Vegan cheese on toast, vegetable sticks	Lentil balls and broad bean purée
Mushrooms on toast	Pesto spiral pasta, cucmber sticks	Tofu scramble, potato cakes
Fruit smoothie bowl	Tartex and cucumber sandwich	Brown noodles with vegetables
Scrambled tofu with vegetables or scrambled eggs	Cheese & watercress sandwich	Pasta with buttermato sauce
Tortilla with peppers	Hummus and carrot sandwich	Cauliflower cheese, green beans
Soya yoghurt with fruit purée	Cream cheese sandwich with cucumber	Rainbow risotto

Breakfast	Lunch	Dinner
Baby bircher muesli	Carrot sticks and hummus	Borlotti bean and carrot purée
Porridge gets fruity	Saksuka with brown rice	Aubergine purée with rice cakes
Coconut yoghurt with apricot purée	Red pepper and tomato purée or soup	Mushrooms on toast with veg fingers
Baby oats with pear purée	Green bean purée	Fruit purée
Toast with nut butter	Broad bean hummus	Scrambled egg or tofu, quinoa
Banana toast	Vegetable crudites with bean dip	Tofu tortilla with mixed vegetable sand chickpeas
Warming cinnamon porridge	Lentil dip with pitta sticks	Scrambled tofu with peppers and onions
Mini tofulettes	Savoury muffins	Spinach and potato purée
Baby buckwheat pancakes	Mixed vegetable couscous	Fennel and apple purée with dill
Apricot yoghurt pots	Parsnip and cream cheese dip with soft veg sticks	Macaroni cheese with steamed veg
Smoothie bowl	Easy hummus, carrot and pepper	Avocado pesto spiral pasta

Breakfast	Lunch	Dinner
Buckwheat pancakes with banana slices	Spinach and potato purée	Roasted red pepper, cashew and cauliflower
Fruit compote with ground rice breakfast	Mini vegan quiche with green beans	Avocado smash
Chia with blueberries	Sunshine Squash	Butternut squash, cauliflower and cannellini beans
Spinach purée	Wraps with black beans and tomato	Pasta with tomato sauce
Avocado smash with toppings	Carrot and courgette muffins	Home made baked beans and potato latkes
Home made beans	Creamy squash and carrot	Baby caponata
Layered chia pudding	Pitta and dips	Lentil stew
Mini strawberry pancakes	Scrambled tofu	Swedish style balls
Saksuka with toast sticks	Felafel and hummus with pitta sticks	Banana pancakes
Warming cinnamon porridge	Green goodness	Rainbow risotto

Breakfast	Lunch	Dinner
Fruit compote	Pumpkin muffins	Vegan baby burger with cucumber sticks
Soya yoghurt with fruit purée	Broad beans and cream cheese on toast	Banana Pancakes
Avocado smash with toppings	Granola bars and apple sauce	Nut rissoles
Fruit smoothie bowl	Bun in the oven pizza	Vegan sausages with veg
Baby bircher muesli	Cashew and lentil bake	Caponata
Home made baked beans	Cauliflower cheese, green beans	Mini bun pizza
Fruit compote with coconut yoghurt	Macaroni cheese with steamed carrots	Macaroni cheese
Layered chia pudding	Mini tofulettes	Lentil stew
Tortilla with peppers	Hummus and carrot sandwich	Stuffed cabbage leaves
Baby buckwheat pancakes	Roasted red pepper, cashew and cauliflower	Fennel and apple purée with dill

Allergen Chart

These are the most common allergens found in food. Many are not found in a vegan or vegetarian diet but it's good to be aware of them.

Sesame and sesame seeds
Peanuts
Gluten / wheat
Mustard
Nuts
Sulphurdioxide and Sulphites
Celery
Milk
Soya
Molluscs
Crustaceans
Eggs
Fish
Lupin

Symptoms of allergies

Watch for the following reactions in your child, especially after introducing a new food.

- Raised, red spots or patches (hives)
- The skin is red, flushed and there is a rash
- The lips, tongue or face is swollen
- They have vomiting and / or diarhhoea
- The child's breathing becomes faster, slower or more difficult or is wheezy, or they have a cough
- They lose consiousness

Remember: that your little one is unable to communicate with you, so you must be able to notice signs that something's not right. You know your baby best, so if you think that something is wrong, act on your instincts.

You do not need to avoid peanuts in pregnancy and it is not thought that eating peanuts in preganancy will reduce your child's likelihood of having a peanut allergy. However, it is advised that you introduce small amounts of peanut products from six months.

Index

Printed in Great Britain
by Amazon

57177221R00083